THE BURNOUT
CURE

THE BURNOUT CURE

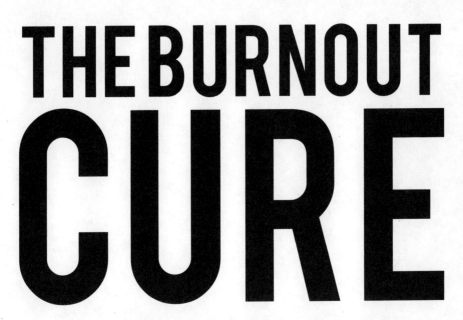

An Emotional Survival Guide
for Overwhelmed Women

JULIE DE AZEVEDO HANKS, MSW, LCSW

Covenant Communications, Inc.

Burnout © Eyewave, istockphotography.com. *Julie de Azevedo Hanks Portrait* by Russ Dixon.

Cover design copyright © 2013 by Covenant Communications, Inc.

Published by Covenant Communications, Inc.
American Fork, Utah

Printed in the United States of America
First Printing: August 2013

19 18 17 16 15 14 13   10 9 8 7 6 5 4 3 2 1

ISBN-13: 978-1-62108-402-0

CONTENTS

You made wine from water
And raised up Jairus's daughter from her bed
Filled the empty fishing nets
And with some loaves and fishes fed
A hungry crowd
Make enough of me to go around

— Julie de Azevedo Hanks

ACKNOWLEDGMENTS

You would not be reading this book were it not for the consistent support of my loving husband, Jeff, and our four wonderful children. They have generously supported me in so many areas of life that have contributed to this book. I am truly blessed and buoyed up by their love.

Many thanks to Jana Erickson and Laurel Christenson for lighting a fire under me to carve out time to write this book, and to Kathy Gordon, Robby Nichols, and the Covenant team for keeping the fire alive.

Thank you to my friend Matt Jackson and my sister Rebecca Overson who provided invaluable feedback and much-needed encouragement during the writing and editing process. Also, thanks to my friends and family for traveling with me through the ups and downs of this book-writing journey.

My heart is full of gratitude for the thousands of women who've shared their hearts with me over the past several years through meaningful discussions about our common struggles as LDS women. These enlightening conversations have helped me to tease out the cultural myths and doctrinal truths presented in this book and have enabled me to raise my voice for the importance of self-care and emotional health in applying true doctrine. The perspectives and insights of my mother, my sisters, my dear friends, my therapy colleagues, my therapy clients, and the Preventing Emotional Burnout workshop and survey participants are woven throughout this book.

I am grateful to my "goodly" parents for being incredibly loving and always supportive, instilling in me a desire to make a difference for good. I'm also thankful that they were wise enough to send me to a therapist as an adolescent, setting me on a journey toward emotional awareness that has brought me a more fulfilling and rich life than I might have had otherwise.

I want to express love to my Heavenly Father for His infinite love and His perfect plan of growth, and to Jesus Christ for showing boundless love and mercy through His life and sacrifice.

PREFACE

ONE OF THE GREAT STRUGGLES we often face as women in the LDS Church whose lives are full of charity for others is avoiding personal emotional burnout.

As a person with strong interests and varied passions, I tend to take on many worthy endeavors simultaneously. For example, while writing this book, I also have responsibilities and commitments as a wife and mother, a gospel doctrine teacher, a performing songwriter, a blogger, media contributor, business consultant, public speaker, and the owner and director of a therapy clinic. These are all good pursuits; I derive much joy and my soul is strengthened by what I do. However, at times, I do—or feel as though I do—try to do *too much*. It seems that I'm always teetering somewhere between exhilaration and exhaustion. Emotional burnout is a topic I know well.

I want to make a difference for good in every aspect of my life—especially in the lives of others. Tuning in to the Spirit and being aware of my own emotions and needs allows me to prioritize and accomplish the things that are important to me and that I feel called to do. Heavenly Father seems to have put many things in my heart that bring me great joy, yet each of them comes with a price. Prayerful guidance from the Spirit helps tutor me in what endeavors should take top priority in my life right now.

My commitment to the gospel and to my family has been and will always be a priority, which often leaves me feeling like engaging with the rest of the "good" aspects of my life is like taking on an impossible juggling act. The only way I can manage to make my abundant life work in a healthy way is to tune in to the Spirit, stay aware of my own emotional needs, and constantly sort through priorities as they shift and change and as I strive to serve others. My hope and prayer is that the insights and tools I offer in this book can help women of the Church who are feeling emotionally drained or just plain exhausted and overwhelmed to find peace and strength, as I have in my life.

My experience as a psychotherapist for nearly two decades has shaped me and provided the basis for many of the insights in this book. I'm amazed by the many bright, good, committed women who pour out their hearts to me about "not feeling good enough" or about feeling like a failure because of the so-called imperfections and struggles that brought them into therapy. By comparing themselves to other women in their family, ward, and neighborhood, the typical women I counsel are battling feelings of discouragement and worthlessness about their performance in life. These types of comparisons are often filled with a focus on the apparent flawless high standard that we seem to see in others while being painfully aware of each and every shortcoming we might have.

Discouragement is one of Satan's greatest tools and is frequently accompanied by serious issues such as chronic exhaustion, depression, fear, worry, anxiety, resentment, confusion, and self-doubt. These emotions are expressed regularly in therapy sessions by women who appear to "have it all together" on the outside but who are suffering quietly on the inside.

Before proceeding further, I want to make clear that I believe strongly in the divine principles of charity, especially charity expressed as Christ-like service. Living Christ-centered lives of service can strengthen us in every aspect of our lives. There is real power in the paradoxical statement that it is only by losing ourselves that we find ourselves. But let's look at this statement a bit more closely. The scripture often quoted is found in Matthew 10:39, and the precise wording is very important for my purposes in this book: "He that findeth his life shall lose it: and he that loseth his life for my sake shall find it." The key to this phrasing is losing our lives *for the Lord's sake*; that is, getting lost in living a Christ-centered life. Of course "finding our lives" in the secular sense results in a selfish and empty life; while this is certainly a problem in our world, it not the focus of this book. This book is focused on helping those of us who have perhaps lost ourselves completely in the service of others and are exhausted to the point that we can no longer find, nourish, care for, and strengthen ourselves so that we might be more effective in continued service of others. The goal of this book is to help us learn how to live lives full of compassion and service for others as we wisely care for ourselves.

My first experience with an overwhelmed woman was long before I became a therapist. My mom, while a generous and unconditionally loving woman who was fiercely dedicated to her role of wife and mother, was frequently overwhelmed by the demands of her life. Married at nineteen, she and my dad quickly started a family, leaving little time for her to realize—let alone explore—what her own needs were. She set out to raise her family, support my dad in his professional endeavors, and serve faithfully in the Church—all of which she did well for decades. My parents raised nine children together. Understandably, my mom didn't have much time to take care of her own needs.

As the second oldest of nine children, I did my share of caretaking. I also unknowingly took on a sense of responsibility for my mom's happiness and well-being by being helpful, obedient, cheerful, and self-sufficient as I tried to lighten her load and ease her bouts of depression. Because of my concern for my mom, I put my own emotional and personal development on hold to some degree.

In my early teens, I began to wonder if it was possible for a faithful Latter-day Saint woman to be a great wife and mom, have a strong and lov-ing family, *and* remain committed to her own personal growth, talents, and interests. While I am incredibly grateful for my mother's sacrifice to raise her family, I had stirrings in my heart that a different life was in store for me. On the deepest level, this book is an expression of the continuing culmination of my journey of building a bridge between what I experienced through my mom's example of adulthood and my own desire to expand on the possibili-ties that awaited me as a woman.

My personal and professional experience has given me great empathy for the struggles that many women face—not only because I too am a woman of faith wife, and mother, but because I've also been in therapy myself. The road I have walked and continue to walk with many clients has led me to discover several wonderful insights that I long to shout from the mountaintops to my sisters in the gospel and to busy women everywhere.

After hearing women express similar feelings of inadequacy, depression, and shame for having problems, I realized that it would be helpful to create a way for all women to hear their feelings echoed and to realize as a result that they are not alone in their struggles.

So I created a workshop ten years ago to present to my own ward that I hoped would address some of the most pervasive issues head-on and give women some emotional freedom and peace of mind. I called the workshop "Preventing Emotional Burnout." I wanted to facilitate a dialogue about common misinterpretations of gospel principles and the fusion of Mormon culture with true doctrine that can keep us feeling stuck in impossible situ-ations—situations in which we find ourselves spread and stretched too far. Most importantly, I wanted to engage some of our common assumptions about who we are and what is required and expected of us as women with a divine inheritance, purpose, and future.

When I first presented the workshop, I created a short survey based on both my clinical observations and personal experiences. I listed the emotional themes I'd observed repeatedly with my clients and created a handful of true/false and short-answer questions. That somewhat last-minute survey ended up being a very powerful tool in revealing the real issues with which many women struggle.

With each subsequent workshop, I sent out the survey in advance and asked the women to complete and return it beforehand, allowing me time to compile statistics for each group. A handful of surveys were administered online, but the bulk of the surveys were handwritten.

I hoped that by presenting the statistical data or survey results of the particular group to whom I was scheduled to speak, I could help normalize the feelings and challenges that *those* women were facing and could open an honest dialogue among them. I wanted each woman to hear the message loud and clear: "You are not alone in your struggles! You are not the only one suffering! We all need help and support!" and, "We can do it with the Lord's help!" I also hoped that the women attending the workshop would continue to be more open with each other and find safety, comfort, and relief in their relationships with other women.

The workshop addressed myths and misinterpretations I had witnessed in Latter-day Saint culture, and I have included the same myths in this book. I believe these myths can perpetuate the feeling of "I'm never good enough." I aim to dispel those myths and help provide a healthy perspective of who we *really* are and what God *actually* expects of us. I've found that what we expect of ourselves or what we *think* God expects of us might actually be quite different from the true, divine, and reassuring reality that you'll find in the scriptures and the teachings of our modern-day prophets. We might find that we are making our lives much harder than they need to be!

Note: While the concepts in this book are directed toward members of The Church of Jesus Christ of Latter-day Saints, they also apply to women—and, indeed, men!—of all faiths. I invite all readers to adapt these concepts and principles in meaningful ways to their own lives.

INTRODUCTION
BURNOUT DEFINED

Burnout IS A STATE OF EXHAUSTION and lack of motivation due to prolonged stress or frustration. It's that persistent feeling of trying really hard but not getting the desired results. Psychologist Herbert Freudenberger, who coined the word *burnout*, defines it as "the extinction of motivation or incentive, especially where one's devotion to a cause or relationship fails to produce the desired results" (Douglas Martin, "Herbert Freudenberger, 73, Coiner of 'Burnout' Is Dead," *New York Times*, December 5, 1999). I love this definition because the word *devotion* so accurately describes what women feel toward their families and their faith. There are certain promises and blessings that we believe we will receive if we are obedient to God's laws. If we do X, then Y will happen. Burnout occurs when we do X and we never get the desired Y, or we get some other undesired result—Z—instead, which could be something unexpected. We might perceive that we have gotten "nothing."

Emotional burnout, as I am describing and using the term here, is not simply the failed results of devotion to a cause. I would extend my definition to include the perception of a failure to attain certain results, successes, blessings, and rewards after devoting all of one's time, talents, and energies to reaching those goals. In other words, at times emotional burnout may be quite formulaic and seem fairly objective. There are many other times (and this is part of what I want to bring to light) when emotional burnout is a very real result of a process that is rather complex, is not very clear, and is based primarily on the individual's subjective perception of herself and her situation. This *does not* make emotional burnout any less real; it's just harder to see and define, not just for herself, but also for those around her.

A client once talked with me about how she had tried so hard to be a dedicated mother and had tirelessly had family prayer, family scripture study, and family home evening (her version of X). She cried as she described to me her feelings of burnout and failure as a mother. Her adult son, who had recently returned from a mission, had left the Church, and she was heartbroken. She had done the *X* (prayer, scriptures, FHE), so she believed that she would get *Y* (a son who stayed faithful to the Church). She had worked so hard for a desired result that had not come.

While this example may seem somewhat simple and formulaic and has the obvious flaw of not taking into account the son's agency, I believe this is a good example to which most of us can relate in some way. Because of that, I think it's useful in opening a discussion about emotional burnout. I say this because on the one hand I see the astonishing beauty of the infinite uniqueness and individuality of women's eternal souls every day. On the other hand, given the differences and innumerable variations in our lives, I see that we are sisters with so much in common as we strive toward similar goals and strive to conquer common obstacles in working out our salvation.

One additional note on the concept of emotional burnout as I am using it throughout the book: while I am focusing on the "emotional" aspect of burnout in our lives, I realize that our feelings and emotional well-being are directly and inseparably connected to our intellectual, social, physical, and, most vitally, our spiritual well-being. The way these aspects of our lives work for each of us is different, but the result I see all too often is the same: emotional burnout. So as we focus on emotions, keep the other aspects of your life in mind, and we will discuss some of them as we work our way through the concepts and exercises in this book.

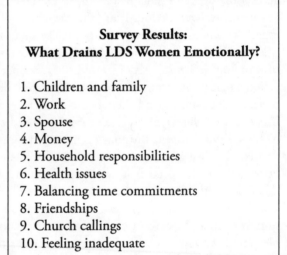

**Survey Results:
What Drains LDS Women Emotionally?**

1. Children and family
2. Work
3. Spouse
4. Money
5. Household responsibilities
6. Health issues
7. Balancing time commitments
8. Friendships
9. Church callings
10. Feeling inadequate

*Helpful Hint: My hope is that you find as many ways as you can to engage with this book, so feel free to write in the margins, fill in the blanks, copy the pages and paste them in your journal, or keep a companion notebook in which you can express your thoughts and feelings as you are prompted.

Take a moment and reflect on how and why parts of your life—even the good parts—can take an emotional toll on you.

Faulty Spiritual Equations and Myths

In my personal and professional life I've observed that much of the emotional burnout in our lives can be attributed to faulty spiritual equations. Regardless of whether we are consciously aware of our belief in faulty spiritual equations, our relentless work and commitment to them creates burnout. Though the scriptures are filled with amazing promises for the followers of Christ, there are actually very few specific and *concrete* blessings promised to us in this life!

In other words, the righteous are promised comfort; "peace in this world, and eternal life in the world to come" (D&C 59:23); and that the "windows of heaven" will be opened (3 Ne. 24:10). The scriptures *don't* say that if you read the scriptures daily and attend church meetings regularly all your children will remain active in the Church. What they *do* say is that you will be blessed with peace, comfort, and eternal life, even though your life today might not look as you imagined it would. Based on my own life experience and my work with numerous women, I believe you may find it helpful to examine your own spiritual equations to see if any of them are faulty or based on myths. This includes slight misunderstandings or applications of true doctrines or beliefs in half-truths and

> Myth: Blessings are always comfortable and feel good.
> Truth: "For whom the Lord loveth he chasteneth" (Heb. 12:6). He allows us to experience adversity and affliction.

"mostly-truths." Erroneous interpretation and application of gospel principles may certainly be contributing to feelings of being "burned out."

However, even living gospel truths to the best of our ability does not make us exempt from adversity. Have you noticed that most of God's beloved prophets experienced intense loss, discomfort, misfortune, and grief throughout their righteous lives? Joseph of Egypt was righteous, but he was thrown into a pit and sold into slavery by his brothers. Nephi was righteous, yet his brothers were constantly tormenting and threatening him. Moses and Lehi were prophets of God, but they wandered in the wilderness—for years—with large groups of murmuring people. The prophet Abinadi taught truths to his people, but King Noah had him burned to death.

Our modern-day prophet Joseph Smith buried six of his children, was tarred and feathered numerous times, and was imprisoned several times—for months at a time—before he was killed by a mob while in Carthage Jail. While in Liberty Jail, the Lord comforted Joseph Smith by reminding him of the immediate promise of peace and the long-term promise of exaltation. He didn't promise a concrete result. The Lord said: "My son, peace be unto thy soul; thine adversity and thine afflictions shall be but a small moment; And then, if thou endure it well, God shall exalt thee on high; thou shalt triumph over all thy foes. Thy friends do stand by thee, and they shall hail thee again with warm hearts and friendly hands" (D&C 121:7–9).

If you find yourself feeling shameful about the fact that you have trials and sufferings, remember that the Lord's prophets experienced much hardship. So you can pretty much count on having afflictions! However, the Lord *has* promised that He will bestow on His followers feelings of peace, increased strength, hope, forgiveness, and mercy to help us through adversity.

As you read and process your thoughts through this book, you will find that there are many reasons for trials and adversity, some of which are not the direct result of our own actions. Some of the pain and suffering in our lives is caused by others, and some of it can be chalked up to "accidents" or just the hazards

> # Myth: If I am experiencing pain in my life it must because of sin.
>
> ## Truth: While pain can be a result of sin, pain isn't always *caused* by sin. Painful "growth" experiences are a necessary part of the plan. Even the righteous— and it appears *especially* the righteous—will experience all kinds of trials and suffering.

of being an imperfect person in an imperfect world. You will find, however, that there will be just as many coping mechanisms as you need to get you through those challenges. One of the most beautiful and amazing aspects of the Atonement is that through its power we can be healed from all types of pain, regardless of its source.

You Are Not Alone

Throughout this book we will untangle some of the cultural myths and faulty beliefs that keep us feeling burned out, exhausted, and "never good enough." Many of the myths became apparent to me after talking to the women who came to the clinic for help or who shared with me during the workshop.

Which of the common cultural myths do *you* believe? Do any of the following sound familiar? Mark and comment on those that apply.

Blessings are always comfortable and feel good.

If I am experiencing pain in my life it must because of sin.

I'm the only one who struggles with _____.

I should be happy all of the time.

Certain emotions are either acceptable or unacceptable to have, show, and talk about.

I should always say yes to reasonable requests.

I have to lose myself completely to find myself.

Struggling with emotional, mental, or relationship problems is a sign of personal or spiritual weakness.

If I'm righteous enough, my family will be perfect.

If we don't talk about things, they aren't real.

Taking good care of myself is selfish.

The people that love me will make sure I'm happy.

My worth is based on my righteousness and performance.

If I notice good things about myself I am being prideful.

I should be perfect now, and perfect means flawless.

Asking for help means I'm weak.

Going to counseling is a sign of spiritual or personal weakness.

Christ will help me only after I've done everything I can.

After seven or eight years of individually surveying every group I spoke to—thousands of women—I noticed that no matter where I went, the results were surprisingly consistent and gave a fairly accurate snapshot for each subsequent group of women. I have surveyed women all over the state of Utah and in several other states as well. It turns out that my hunch was right: Our feelings about ourselves, our fears about being selfish, and our ambivalence about where emotional self-care fits into our lives are prevalent whether we live in Hawaii, California, or Utah. (I've yet to be invited to speak outside the United States, but I suspect that the statistics may not vary too drastically for women in other parts of the world.)

I am always touched by the honest and courageous answers offered in the survey and especially in the workshop itself. I am, however, greatly troubled by the apparent correlation between a fear of appearing to "care for ourselves" and resulting emotional burnout.

One of the prevailing and pernicious themes that arises from many of these comments is a vicious cycle of feeling discouraged or depressed about not doing enough good in the world around us and that the only or best way to make ourselves feel better is to do more for others. This type of behavior most often

Myth: I'm the only one who struggles.
Truth: You are not alone. We all experience painful times as part of being in a fallen world.

leads to running faster than we have strength, spreading ourselves too thin, and experiencing emotional burnout. The truth, as King Benjamin taught, is that while it is "expedient that we be diligent" it is not "requisite" that we run "faster than we have strength." He exhorts us to do all things in "wisdom and order" (Mosiah 4:27). I hope to help you learn that a healthy balance between aspects of proper self-care is essential to the goals of doing more good for others—which makes all of us feel good!

I encourage you to complete—as openly and honestly as you can—the "Preventing Emotional Burnout" survey (there's a brief form below, in addition to a photocopy format in the appendix). Especially if you're really struggling, it may help to repeat the survey after implementing some of the principles and tools in this book. Repeat the survey as frequently and as often as you like; a running record of the results may help you highlight your areas or progress and help you see where there's room for improvement. As you proceed through this book and do the exercises, I hope you'll understand that you are not alone in your struggles—and that you will discover how to take better care of yourself so you have more to offer to your Heavenly Father and to your earthly relationships.

Preventing Emotional Burnout Survey

I have enough time to pursue my own interests and needs.	T	F
I often take on more commitments than I can handle.	T	F
I say "no" when someone asks me to do something that I don't want to do.	T	F
I often feel guilty about all of the things that I am not doing.	T	F
It is easier to give help than to accept help from others.	T	F
I am comfortable expressing anger, frustrations, and disappointment.	T	F
I have struggled at one time or another with emotional or mental health problems (depression, anxiety, low self-esteem, abuse, substance abuse, etc.).	T	F
Family members have struggled with emotional problems.	T	F
I get less than seven hours of sleep every night.	T	F
I exercise at least three times per week for half an hour at a time.	T	F
I am generally happy with my life and relationships.	T	F
I can easily accept compliments from others.	T	F
I am tired or worried most of the time.	T	F
I have sought professional counseling.	T	F
If so, for what reasons?		
Family members have sought professional counseling.	T	F
If so, for what reasons?		
I have considered going to counseling, but I haven't followed through.	T	F
If so, what has prevented me from seeking help?		
The areas of my life that are the most emotionally draining for me are:		
The thing I would most like to change about myself is:		

How to Use this Book

I have two rules as you continue to proceed through this book. The first rule: *This book is a guilt-free experience!* I am going to make a compelling case for the need for you to take better care of yourself—remembering, of course, that this is not an argument to completely abandon your responsibilities for others. I will give you six concrete suggestions for preventing emotional burnout:

1. Feel and express a full range of emotions.
2. Give yourself permission to say an inspired "no."
3. Do your emotional family history.
4. Take responsibility for your own happiness.
5. Practice being kind to yourself.
6. Learn to ask for and accept help.

Do not—I repeat, *do not* take these six things and add them to your already never-ending list of things to do! You know the list I'm talking about—the one we all have that includes any or all of the following: bake twelve loaves of bread for the neighborhood daily, get up every morning at 5 A.M. to exercise for two hours, volunteer at the food bank, read scriptures three hours a day, do your genealogy back to Adam and Eve, keep the house (and garage and yard) sparkling clean, prepare a PowerPoint presentation for your child's Primary talk, go to every temple in the United States this year, grow a weed-free garden, and so on. That's the list I'm talking about. Don't use these six suggestions to make that list any longer! I am not offering another reason to feel guilty about what you might not be doing—especially things that are less essential to your salvation.

My whole purpose is to lighten your load by offering my best personal and professional suggestions—helpful points of view, if you will—that have made a big difference in my own life and in the lives of many women I've counseled. If something you read here touches your heart, great! Take that one thing and apply it if you want to. Or not! If nothing resonates with you, that's fine too. At the very minimum, you'll have more tools to apply in your life if you ever need them, or you can share these tools with others.

The second rule is this: *Participate!* Reading this book is very much like attending one of my workshops. You can hang out in the back row and wait for refreshments to be served, or you can lean forward with your heart on the line and pull the information toward you to expand your view of life. I invite you to engage in meaningful exploration and actually *do* the exercises.

I will also invite you to pause and reflect on aspects of your life throughout this book. Please *do* stop and answer the questions, even if you can't bring yourself to actually write them in this workbook. Consider deepening your commitment to take good care of yourself as you discover what feelings, beliefs, mindsets, and activities will help you on your journey.

The Emotional Oxygen Mask

The following analogy struck a chord with me as to why taking care of ourselves is critically important if we desire to truly lift, serve, and support others. Several years ago I was on a flight to Los Angeles to do some vocal recording sessions. I was holding my son Owen, who was then six months old. I have been on commercial flights many times in my life, and like many passengers, tend to tune out the flight attendants as they explain the safety information. With genuine concern for the young baby in my arms, I thought, *I'd better listen this time.*

The flight attendant started talking about what to do if there were a change in cabin pressure. She said, "The oxygen masks will drop from the ceiling and oxygen will begin to flow. Place your mask on first and then assist others, such as small children or the elderly."

Did she really just say that—put your own mask on *first?* Was this new information I had somehow missed dozens of times before? As I sat in the plane holding my precious little baby, I realized that my instinct as a woman, as a parent, would be to make sure that my little son and everyone else in my row got an oxygen mask *first.* But this time I clearly heard the flight attendant's message: Put on *your own* mask first and then assist others! I realized what she was really saying: If I don't put my oxygen mask on first, I'll pass out—and what good am I going to be to my six-month-old if I'm passed out on the floor?

What a great analogy for our emotional lives. As women, isn't it true that our instinct is to respond to the needs of others, to put their needs first at the expense of our own? And then what happens?

I see a lot of exhausted, overwhelmed, confused women in my life and in my practice—women who are emotionally "passed out on the floor"—not necessarily because of all they have to do, but because of a failure to include themselves in all the nurturing they are doing. In the name of service, they nurture others first, but they do so at the *expense* of nurturing themselves and by neglecting their own emotional needs.

No matter where I've presented my "Preventing Emotional Burnout" workshops through the years, I've always felt at home. That might be because there is almost always a lovely lace tablecloth and something chocolate to eat afterward! (I just love that aspect of Relief Society!) All kidding aside, when I am with Relief Society women, I am always reassured that I am not alone in my struggles and that I'm truly part of a worldwide sisterhood of women who are sincerely striving to be like the Savior. It is my prayer that by reading this book and pondering its message you will begin to see the importance of taking good care of yourself so there is more of you to offer in the service of others, especially in those relationships that matter most to you.

CURE 1: FEEL AND EXPRESS A FULL RANGE OF EMOTIONS

Feelings Are Like Colors

I LIKE TO COMPARE THE spectrum of human emotions to colors—not just to the red, yellow, green, blue, and violet the human eye sees in a common rainbow, but to a painter's palette with hundreds to thousands of colors differing in value, saturation, and hue. Like that incredible range of color, we have unlimited access to feelings of many shades and varieties. Unfortunately, early on in life many of us are trained to believe that only certain emotions are acceptable. Maybe you got the message that it's only okay to feel happy, or to be nice, or to be brave, polite, or humble. But that's like getting stuck with only four or five colors with which to paint your life when you are actually capable of feeling and expressing so much more than that.

Consider your beliefs for a moment. You hold certain spiritual beliefs because you *feel* them in your heart. You love your friends because you *feel* affection or are drawn to them. You take care of your family because you have a strong commitment coupled with an emotional bond. Our feelings are a crucial aspect of who we are, regardless of whether we are aware of those feelings.

Learning to identify and express a *full* range of emotions is the basic foundation for emotional self-care. Your feelings give valuable clues to guide you, and they provide you with information about your unique preferences, passions, and personality. Our emotions are not only a vital source of information but are the glue that cements us to one another and to God. But most of us limit ourselves in our ability to acknowledge and express our feelings to ourselves and to others.

Developing a sense of emotional awareness and expression is a really important part of preventing burnout! You have to be able to first know what you are feeling; allow yourself to feel it; and then figure out how to learn from, effectively handle, and appropriately express those emotions. Being able to understand, appreciate, and share what you are feeling is a huge component of human intimacy. If you want to truly connect with those who matter most to you, you'll have to expand your emotional "palette."

Energy in Motion

I find that it's helpful to think of emotions as E-MOTIONS, or Energy-in-Motion. If we think of emotions as energy that moves us to take action, or moves us toward a greater awareness, or moves us toward growth, it's easier to remove feelings out of the automatic "good–bad" or "positive–negative" categories we assign them out of habit. Feelings are not inherently good or bad; they are simply *information* to help guide us through our earthly experience.

If emotions are energy in motion, it's important to realize that we have some control over our emotions and can learn to direct them as that emotional energy moves *through* us. Ultimately, emotional energy needs to go somewhere. Sadly, unacknowledged and

---

**Workshop Comments:
Keeping My Emotions In**

Here's what workshop participants said when asked the question, *What happens when you don't acknowledge and express difficult emotions?*

—Those emotions get trapped inside and fester.
—My blood pressure rises.
—I get stressed out.
—I get headaches.
—I tend to overeat.
—I withdraw and get depressed.
—I start worrying.
—I get really irritable.
—I feel on the verge of tears all the time.
—I take it out on my kids.
—After a while I blow up at someone who doesn't deserve it.

---

unrestrained negative emotions often move through us without much control and can do great harm to us, especially our interpersonal relationships and even our relationship with God. We'll talk about controlling our emotional expressions and actions more below. But an important question to think about now is, *What happens when that emotional energy doesn't have a place to go?* What happens when we shut down, numb out, hold it in, or pretend those feelings are not there?

Pause and Reflect: Difficult Emotions

What emotions do you have a hard time acknowledging or expressing?

_____

_____

_____

What happens to you when you don't express emotions?

_____

_____

_____

What behaviors do you engage in when you are trying not to feel something you are feeling?

_____

_____

_____

What signs does your body give you that you're not dealing with your feelings?

_____

_____

_____

Emotions Aren't Inherently Good or Bad

We teach our children at a very early age to identify colors because it is a basic step toward understanding and relating to the world around them. We teach our children that apples are red, the sky is blue, the night sky is black, and frogs are green. Recalling the previous discussion of colors, how many colors of apples are there (consider how many colors there are in a single apple)? How many amazing shades of color have we seen in the sky, day or night? And did you know that frogs not only are various shades of green, but also red, orange, yellow, black and white, and even blue!

Extending this analogy, how much time do we spend time teaching our children how to accurately label their emotions—especially difficult or mixed feelings? Do we say, "Wow, you look upset right now!" or "Honey, you are really excited about that!" Most of us weren't encouraged to identify our emotions at an early age, and even fewer were taught how express emotions powerfully and effectively. It's no wonder that we are limited in how we can talk about feelings as adults; we learned as children that we had to be, feel, and act a certain way in particular situations in order to get the love, approval, or attention we wanted.

If you are like me, you most likely learned that certain feelings were acceptable or good, and others were unacceptable or bad. Naturally, we want to feel more of the *good* feelings and avoid the *bad* ones. I don't know if you've noticed yet, but our journey in life presents us with a full range of experiences that elicit

Myth: Certain emotions are either acceptable or unacceptable to have, show, and talk about.

Truth: Emotions aren't necessarily good or bad. Emotions are simply energy in motion that offers vital information to guide our lives.

from us many different emotions—joy, discomfort, pain, fear, excitement, and distress. While we do have some control over how we react to certain emotions, we don't always get to pick and choose the ones we experience. Even if we live our lives as best we can and try to make all the right choices, despair or frustration or heartache will still find us—even the best of us.

It is always touching to read the "Psalm of Nephi" where this beloved and righteous prophet of God openly and honestly admits the pain and suffering this mortal existence can present (see 2 Ne. 4:15–20). In verse 15 Nephi exclaims how his soul delights in the scriptures, his heart ponders them, and he writes them for the profit of others—including us today. In verse 16, Nephi's soul openly delights in the things of the Lord; he continually ponders the amazing things he has seen and heard from the prophets, from the Spirit, and from God Himself. Yet in verse 17 he laments, "Nevertheless, notwithstanding the great goodness of the Lord, in showing me his great and marvelous works, my heart exclaimeth: O wretched man that I am! Yea, my heart sorroweth because of my flesh; my soul grieveth because of mine iniquities." In verse 18 he openly admits that he is so easily beset (assailed and harassed) by temptations and sins that surround him.

In a manner I believe is similar to so many of us, in verse 19 he states that just as he desires to rejoice, his heart groans because of his sins. But he adds this important rejoinder: "nevertheless, I know in whom I have trusted." And he continues in verse 20, "My God hath been my support; he hath led me through mine afflictions in the wilderness; and he hath preserved me upon the waters of the great deep." What a magnificent and emotionally honest testimony of a life of faith, courage, power, and long-suffering that is centered precisely where it should be—on Christ.

Consider the possibility that life is about growth, not about comfort. Those who seek comfort—those who try to maximize the good feelings and squash the bad ones—are likely living life with an emotional dishonesty that will eventually bring more pain. If my goal is to live a conveniently comfortable life, I won't take risks, I won't do anything that challenges me, I'll avoid anything unfamiliar, and I'll always wonder why difficult things are still happening to me. However, if I live life from the viewpoint that everything that happens is an opportunity for my growth, I'll be much more willing to participate fully in life and receive whatever the Lord gives me. This, of course, includes a much more satisfying sense of comfort from the Spirit through the power of the Savior's Atonement.

Aside from the numerous scriptural examples of the Lord's prophets and chosen people being faced with many challenges, consider the Savior Himself. He was the only sinless person to walk the earth, yet His life was full of hardship and trials. He was born in a humble stable; shortly thereafter, King Herod mandated the death of every infant boy. Throughout His ministry Christ was threatened and challenged by local rulers, religious leaders, and His people. He was mocked, misunderstood, scorned, tempted, abandoned, betrayed, and tortured. He gave up His life in a public, excruciatingly painful way that is beyond our mortal comprehension. When we say we want to follow the Savior, consider that following Him might also mean that we need to open ourselves up to be willing to experience *all* that life has to offer—not just the comfortable stuff, but the strife and pain too.

I'm not suggesting that you need to seek out discomfort; the discomfort of life's hardships and trials will find you. By following Christ's example as we experience trials and sorrow and pain, we should not fear them but look to God instead; this is often the difference between simply enduring life and enduring it *well*. In the premortal earth life we shouted for joy when we chose to follow the Savior's plan for us to come to earth and have *all* of the experiences available here. Painful experiences are part of being human, and they are critical for our learning and growth. We voted for the privilege of experiencing opposition. Wanting things to be easy was Satan's plan.

Orson F. Whitney said:

> No pain that we suffer, no trial that we experience is wasted. It ministers to our education, to the development of such

qualities as patience, faith, fortitude and humility. All that we suffer and all that we endure, especially when we endure it patiently, builds up our characters, purifies our hearts, expands our souls, and makes us more tender and charitable, more worthy to be called the children of God . . . and it is through sorrow and suffering, toil and tribulation, that we gain the education that we come here to acquire and which will make us more like our Father and Mother in heaven. . . . (Spencer W. Kimball, *Faith Precedes the Miracle* [Salt Lake City: Deseret Book, 1972], 98)

In other words, the pain and sorrow we experience can be just as important as the joy and peace we feel. Remember, we would not feel joy if it were not for the suffering. The valleys and peaks of our soul's journey in this life are inseparably connected.

The Six Basic Emotions

If you don't know exactly what you're feeling or you just don't have a label for it, but know that you feel exhausted or overwhelmed, try going through what I see as six basic emotions and ask yourself, "Do I feel happy, mad, sad, scared, surprised, or disgusted?" Sometimes it feels less overwhelming as you start out to name and narrow complex feelings down to six emotional "colors" or categories. With that, you can get to work with what you have available to you and can make some progress.

You can't always rely on immediate inclinations or outward manifestations to tell you how you or others are feeling. Emotions are very subjective concepts; trying to be objective about them is important but should be approached with care and understanding. For example, if you see me crying you can't assume that I'm sad. When I'm happy, I cry. When I'm sad, I cry. When I'm mad, I cry. When I'm scared, you guessed it—I cry.

The six basic emotions I'm using for our purposes here have been identified cross-culturally by facial expression by psychologist and researcher Paul Ekman. They are as follows:

Happy

Mad

Sad

Scared

Surprised

Disgusted

From those basic six emotional "colors" you can branch out and determine, "Well, I'm happy, but it's more peaceful," or "I'm mad, but disappointed fits better." There are so many words you can use to describe your inner experience and learn more about yourself. Spend some time reflecting and pondering on your emotions; draw from the Spirit to help you understand and express yourself. Add a few minutes a day, perhaps in conjunction with gospel study or prayers, to make note of your emotions. Writing in diaries, journals, letters, or on the computer or even recording your thoughts on a voice recorder (many new phones have this feature) are all great places to make a start. Keeping your own emotional record may prove to be beneficial as you track your progress.

Increase Your Vocabulary to Express Your Feelings

The list below can help you describe your emotions more clearly and add more hues to your emotional landscape; feel free to add others if they occur to you. There is power in naming your feelings. It makes them more real; helps you sort through them and address them in healthier ways instead of ignoring them or letting them overwhelm you; and makes them more manageable.

Happy

Adored	Alive	Appreciated
Cheerful	Ecstatic	Excited
Glad	Grateful	Hopeful
Jolly	Jovial	Joyful
Loved	Merry	Optimistic
Pleased	Satisfied	Tender
Terrific	Thankful	Uplifted
Warm		

Mad

Aggravated	Accused	Angry
Bitter	Cross	Defensive
Frustrated	Furious	Hostile
Impatient	Infuriated	Insulted
Jaded	Offended	Ornery
Outraged	Pestered	Rebellious
Resistant	Revengeful	Scorned
Spiteful	Testy	Used
Violated		

Sad

Alone	Blue	Burdened
Depressed	Devastated	Disappointed
Discouraged	Grief-stricken	Gloomy
Heartbroken	Hopeless	Let down
Lonely	Melancholy	Miserable
Neglected	Pessimistic	Remorseful
Resentful	Solemn	Threatened

Scared

Afraid	Alarmed	Anxious
Bashful	Cautious	Fearful
Frightened	Haunted	Helpless
Hesitant	Horrified	Insecure
Lost	Nervous	Petrified
Puzzled	Reassured	Reserved
Sheepish	Tearful	Uncomfortable
Useless		

Surprised

Astonished	Curious	Delighted
Enchanted	Exhilarated	Incredulous
Inquisitive	Impressed	Mystified
Passionate	Playful	Replenished
Splendid	Shocked	Stunned

Disgusted

Ashamed	Embarrassed	Exposed
Guilty	Ignored	Inadequate
Incompetent	Inhibited	Inept
Inferior	Insignificant	Sick
Squashed	Stupid	Ugly
Unaccepted		

Pause and Reflect: What Are You Feeling Now?

Stop for a moment and check in with your emotional self. Close your eyes. Take a deep breath. Ask yourself what words best describe the emotion you are feeling right now.

_____

_____

_____

_____

I'm Not Supposed to Be Mad

I have a Catholic colleague and mentor who has worked in Salt Lake City for more than thirty years. I once asked her, "What's the most unique, peculiar thing about working with LDS clients?"

She said, "They don't get mad. They don't even want to *recognize* when they're mad."

> # Myth: I should be happy all of the time.
> # Truth: No one I know feels happy all the time. Even Christ experienced a full range of emotion.

To feel anger is to be human. My personal and clinical experiences support my colleague's notion that Latter-day Saints do not really know what to do with their anger when it comes up. Some mistakenly believe that the only way to express anger is by screaming, shouting, losing control, or being physically or emotionally violent, so they want to avoid anger altogether. We value being loving, patient, and longsuffering; anger can be hurtful or lead us to do hurtful things. People who believe anger is not okay become adept at various methods of suppressing or hiding the anger they feel, which actually leads to more emotional pain and suffering.

Survey: Can You Express Anger?

Of women surveyed, 54 percent reported they have difficulty expressing anger, frustration, and disappointment.

One of the best ways to ease our burdens—especially our emotional ones—is to expand our ability to express and acknowledge anger in a healthy, constructive way.

Here is an example from my workshop:

> One major issue is that I don't know how to express anger. I
> grew up in a very "angry" house, and I know that words can't
> be taken back. When anger is an attack and a put-down, it
> hurts your heart. You don't want to put anyone else in that
> situation. As a mother, because I saw that, the last thing I
> want do is hurt someone with anger.

Another workshop participant grew up in a home with the opposite
problem:

> I grew up in a home where my mother never expressed an-
> ger. She told me it's not ladylike and that you have to be in
> control all the time. Since it was never okay to express anger
> growing up, I had to hold it in. As an adult I have had to
> work hard to learn how to share my angry feelings and stand
> up for myself so people don't run over me.

Human tendency is to either do what our parents did or to go to the opposite extreme. Both women in the examples above learned to suppress their
anger, which could possibly lead to a new set of unhealthy behaviors. The
usual result is that an attempt to curtail anger—by trying to avoid perceived
pain—leads to more pain!

Finding a healthy way to acknowledge and manage anger is so important for
preventing emotional burnout. When I was growing up there was an understanding in my family that it was not okay to be mad. Anger was labeled as "not Christ-
like" and therefore not okay to express at all. Just like every other human on the
planet, I felt anger—but the message I received was that if I felt anger, I was a "bad
person." So I learned to shut down anger and sadness by obsessing about food and
my body. This led to body image and eating issues. Another way I tried to avoid
anger in myself and at others was to try hard to make everyone else around me
happy. I became an emotional caretaker, and I just couldn't stand to have anyone
mad at anyone else. Later in this chapter I'll offer some suggestions for dealing
with anger in a healthier way. But for now, just realize that it is vitally important to
recognize and acknowledge feelings of anger.

Believe it or not, it's not just the uncomfortable feelings that get shut
down or numbed. Some people also shut down "feel-good" emotions. I've
worked with clients whose families ignored, discounted, or shamed them for
expressing joy or excitement over successes. Imagine a young grade-schooler

running home to share her excitement over her excellent report card with her mom. If her mother responds with, "Wow, are you sure they didn't mix up your report card with Lisa's?" or "Don't brag about that. You'll make your brother feel bad that he didn't get straight As," imagine the discouragement that little girl feels. She may learn to never share for fear of being shut down.

Another reason some people suppress their happiness is that life circumstances have taught them that they just don't matter—period. I've had clients who felt overlooked because another family member was in perpetual crisis, maybe battling chronic health issues or substance abuse. They may have concluded that it wasn't okay to be happy or lighthearted when there was so much hardship in their family.

One-upmanship is another way to muzzle happiness. I once worked with a client whose mother tended to one-up her whenever she shared positive emotions about a work or relationship success. She stopped sharing her joy

---

Workshop Comments: Expressing Anger

The following are some reasons women gave for why they had difficulty expressing anger:

—I am supposed to be nice.
—We think we're the only ones who aren't happy, so we keep it to ourselves.
—We should be the happiest people in the world!
—Humility and anger don't go together, and we should seek to be humble.
—When I feel anger, I don't know how to express it or to whom I should express it.
—I'm trying to be like Jesus. It's hard to be negative and be like Jesus.
—I don't want to hurt someone's feelings.
—I don't want to be known as being "out of control."
—I want people to like me. People don't like to be around negative people.
—It's not ladylike to show anger.
—Showing anger is not Christ-like.

---

and successes as a way to avoid hearing her mother's cutting remarks.

We may also become emotionally burned out when, for some unidentified reason or perhaps due to a combination of reasons, we have felt so exhausted and overwhelmed for so long that we forget to acknowledge and commend or congratulate ourselves for doing something good and for trying to do what is right. There's always a danger of becoming self-righteous or full of one's self. But for those of us whose souls are a bit drained, it is critical to make even the smallest efforts to do good and to allow ourselves to feel genuinely good about our accomplishments—regardless of what the world tells us.

Through my own experience in therapy as a teenager, I discovered for myself that feelings are neither good nor bad—they're simply *feelings*. I also learned the vital lesson of opening up and dealing with difficult emotions as best I could. What a relief it was to discover that I was free to allow myself to feel whatever I was feeling and to learn healthier ways of expressing those emotions!

Pause and Reflect: Expressing Difficult Emotions

Why do you think more than half of women surveyed have difficulty expressing anger, frustration, and disappointment?

_____

_____

_____

What emotions are the most difficult for you to acknowledge or express?

_____

_____

_____

Angry Feelings versus Angry Behavior

Culturally, part of the problem is that many people meld angry *feelings* and angry *behavior*; they often happen so spontaneously and simultaneously that they seem inseparable. But they are actually two separate things! Angry *feelings* give us a clue that something needs to be addressed or attended to. What we *do* with those angry feelings is our choice.

Likewise, angry actions (including thoughts, words, and deeds) underscore the need for serious and thoughtful efforts to understand what underlies those feelings and actions. Part of the problem is that there is not always a clear cause-and-effect relationship between feelings and actions. Sometimes a client tells me that she feels angry when her husband acts in a certain way, and then she blames herself for being upset. More often, however, women I talk to express frustration at demonstrating anger and being troubled that they can't quite pinpoint the source of their anger.

Obviously, confusing our anger with a need to hurt loved ones verbally, emotionally, or physically is damaging and not compatible with the gospel. So how can we learn to recognize anger or other difficult feelings and then find ways to express them productively, honestly, and respectfully?

Here is a personal example of how an angry feeling was expressed in a productive, respectful way. My oldest son played football during his freshman year of high school, and one day he left me the following voicemail: "Mom, I'm really mad at you. You keep taking the chinstrap from my helmet out of the laundry so it never gets washed and I'm getting acne all over my chin! Love you, bye."

He could have come home and yelled at me, thrown his helmet down, and blamed me for his acne. Instead, he simply told me he was feeling angry and let me know what I was doing that upset him. He knows that I was not trying to make his life hard, and I appreciate that he was able to tell me that he was angry. He didn't act rude, and he didn't put me down or insult me. He simply stated the facts. I really appreciated that.

Okay, to be honest, my initial reaction after hearing his voicemail was to feel like an angry martyr. For the first few seconds I thought, *After all I do for you! Wash your stupid chinstrap yourself!* Then I realized he wasn't attacking me. I had coached my son for years to express his emotions directly and responsibly, and that's exactly what he'd done. I called him back and thanked him for telling me how he felt. I also let him know that I was trying to prevent the chinstrap from getting damaged in the wash, but now that I understood what he needed, I would be happy to wash it with the rest of his uniform.

Here's another personal example: In preparation for my very first emotional burnout workshop, my husband, Jeff, offered to help by copying the workshop handout packets during his lunch break that day. He walked in the door after work as I was preparing to head to the meetinghouse to set up for my presentation. When I asked him for the handouts, his face dropped and his eyes widened. "I totally spaced it!" he said, horrified.

You know what my response was? "That's okay." Except that was a lie. It *wasn't* okay, and I was disappointed, but I didn't say that. He said he'd hurry to make copies and bring them to me at the meetinghouse.

As I drove to the meetinghouse, I realized that I was on my way to speak to a group of women on healthy emotional expression—and I realized that I wasn't practicing what I preached. So I called my husband and told him, "You know, it's actually *not* okay with me that you forgot. I was counting on you. I feel mad, and I'm disappointed. And underneath that is some hurt and fear that I'm not important to you. But I know that you didn't mean to forget, and I know you weren't trying to hurt me."

This is an example of how powerful it is to acknowledge and share feelings of anger instead of pretending to be "fine." There was no screaming, yelling, or spewing of accusations or hurtful words. I was feeling anger, and I could see that, and I offered information about my feelings while trying to offer understanding and compassion to him, too. I cannot stress enough that it is not only important to try to manage our own anger, but it's also important to manage our reactions to other people's anger when it's directed at us.

All too often in our world and in our culture, we obsess over being right and become immediately indignant when our character is attacked. We also live in a world filled with examples of retaliation. When someone expresses anger toward us, it is so easy to fire right back, to become defensive, and to throw up walls to protect ourselves or deflect the issue (especially to turn the "blame" back on the other person). Somewhat ironically, these tendencies become increasingly difficult with those we know the best and should love the most; our intimate knowledge of the other person provides us with an arsenal of information to use in emotional combat when that same knowledge could and should be the common ground that leads to increased peace, love, and understanding.

Feelings are an internal experience. By understanding that it is okay to simply feel anger as part of our natural, mortal experience allows us to pause, ponder, and reflect on finding more productive ways of dealing with and expressing anger.

Pause and Reflect: Which Emotions Have Become Off-Limits in Your Life?

What are some emotions you do not share? What are your reasons for not expressing difficult or painful emotions (like anger)?

_____

_____

_____

What did you learn during your childhood about emotions? How did you deal with certain feelings that were off-limits your house?

_____

_____

_____

Rethinking "Christ-like"

Perhaps the single most important doctrinal principle we are commanded to follow in our lives as members of the Church is to try to lead a Christ-like life. While we may not understand fully the eternal meaning of this principle, most of us are painfully aware that this exhortation—difficult as it is at times—will ultimately bring us the greatest joy. It concerns me, though, that there seems to be a cultural belief that to be "Christ-like" means that we should always be nice, sweet, charitable, forgiving, positive, and perpetually happy. I am not suggesting that these are not Christ-like characteristics or that we should not strive to live them. But as a therapist, I've often heard people talk about being Christ-like as synonymous with being nice and happy all of the time.

I'm concerned that this limited belief of what it means to be "Christ-like" does not allow us to experience a full range of emotions and therefore sets us up for emotional dishonesty and disconnect. What I mean by this is that we take the ideal of "trying to be like Jesus" with us into the heat of everyday battle (*as we should*) where we are bound to make some mistakes and fall short of our ideal way of being Christ-like. For some of us this will feel like failure—and this is the problem I want to address. Since we cannot be exactly like Christ in this life, our charge is to be as Christ-like as we can in this mortal existence. I ardently believe that a healthier approach to understanding what it means for us to live a Christ-like life will be enhanced by broadening our view of how we can feel a full range of emotions while being righteous disciples of our Lord and Savior.

No mortal being that I know of feels happy *all* of the time. I can't tell you how many times I ask clients during an initial psychotherapy session how they are feeling, and they calmly reply, "Fine." So my next question is, "If everything is 'fine,' why did you schedule a therapy appointment?" When we believe we are supposed to be nice and happy all the time—without exception—we shut down our full range of emotions and express or acknowledge only "positive" feelings.

The scriptures are full of examples of righteous men and women—and even God Himself—expressing a full range of emotions. The Old Testament indicates that God felt and expressed His anger righteously. The phrase *wrath of God* is used repeatedly in the Old Testament. The Topical Guide to the LDS scriptures also refers readers to look up *anger, fury, indignation,* and *rage.* Here are a few examples:

"The wrath of God came upon them, and slew the fattest of them, and smote down the chosen men of Israel" (Ps. 78:3).

"For which things' sake the wrath of God cometh on the children of disobedience" (Col. 3:6).

"Let no man deceive you with vain words: for because of these things cometh the wrath of God upon the children of disobedience" (Eph. 5:6).

"But the Lord is the true God, he is the living God, and an everlasting king: at his wrath the earth shall tremble, and the nations shall not be able to abide his indignation" (Jer. 10:10).

In the New Testament, John 2:13–16 describes the incident of Christ throwing money-changers out of the temple with a whip by saying He overturned tables and "poured out the changers' money." This seems to be describing someone with deep emotion who was taking a stand against those who were *defiling* His Father's house. He used His emotions *for righteous purposes.* One of the functions of anger is to propel us to action, to take a stand for something or someone in a strong way, the way that Christ took a stand for His Father. Since Christ was sinless, this scriptural account helps illustrate that strong emotion and behavior are not necessarily sins and can be used in accordance with God's will.

In this example, Christ saw something that wasn't right, and He took action to restore integrity. It was the temple, and He cleaned it out. It doesn't say that He screamed and engaged in fist fights. He swiftly removed the people and activities that were defiling His Father's house. I think the closest and simplest example of how this might translate into your life is to imagine how you would feel to walk into your own home and find that your adorable two-year-old had dumped cereal and milk all over the floor and had taken a permanent marker to your freshly painted walls. In your best moment you would probably say, "Hey, sweetie, stop that!" You might pick her up, remove the marker, clean up the mess, and get her focused on something better. In your less-than-shining moments, you might express greater frustration with an angry shout and there might be a slap on the hand or swat on the bottom of her diaper.

No matter how upset we might be in the moment, the scriptures and modern-day prophets are very clear about how we should treat the children in our lives. And this is where we might be able to see that we can use a brief pause and contemplation (a quick prayer always helps) to put the situation into an eternal perspective—into a more Christ-like perspective—and acknowledge and accept our anger and deal with it appropriately. In an effort to correct situations such as this, we sometimes need, on some level, to repent. This would mean asking forgiveness (yes, even from a small child), expressing sorrow, showing forth "an increase of love" as the scriptures admonish us (see D&C 122), and striving to improve our actions and reactions to such situations.

Learning from the Savior's Full Range of Emotion

Throughout the scriptures Christ and those close to Him give glimpses into His emotional life. Here are just a few of the numerous scriptures that suggest that the Savior experienced a broad range of feelings while in mortality.

Compassion: "And he said unto them: Behold, my bowels are filled with compassion towards you" (3 Ne. 17:6).

Anger and grief: "And when he had looked round about on them with anger, being grieved for the hardness of their hearts, he saith unto the man, Stretch forth thine hand. And he stretched it out: and his hand was restored whole as the other" (Mark 3:5).

Love: "We love him, because he first loved us" (1 John 4:19).

Joy: "And they arose from the earth, and he said unto them: Blessed are ye because of your faith. And now behold, my joy is full" (3 Ne. 17:20).

Sorrow: "And saith unto them, My soul is exceeding sorrowful unto death: tarry ye here, and watch" (Mark 14:34).

Indignation: "And it shall come to pass, because of the wickedness of the world, that I will take vengeance upon the wicked, for they will not repent; for the cup of mine indignation is full; for behold, my blood shall not cleanse them if they hear me not" (D&C 29:17).

Fear and trepidation: "And he went a little further, and fell on his face, and prayed, saying, O my Father, if it be possible, let this cup pass from me: nevertheless not as I will, but as thou wilt" (Matt. 26:39).

Forsaken and alone: "My God, my God, why hast thou forsaken me?" (Matt. 27:46).

Agony: "And being in an agony he prayed more earnestly: and his sweat was as it were great drops of blood falling down to the ground" (Luke 22:44).

Being Christlike with Care

Of course, we should all prayerfully study and try to understand to the best of our ability the paramount example of what it means to be "Christlike," especially as we try to comprehend and apply the Atonement in our lives. In the scriptures we read what happened as Jesus was about to embark on the infinite Atonement in the Garden of Gethsemane: "And he taketh with him Peter and James and John, and began to be sore amazed, and to be very heavy; And saith unto them, My soul is exceeding sorrowful unto death: tarry ye here, and watch" (Mark 14:33–34).

We have been given an account of the Atonement and the days that follow both in the scriptures and in numerous commentaries from apostles and prophets; the account of that part of the Savior's life should be included in our studies of how to live a Christ-like life. I am always moved by the numerous and varied examples of emotion that Christ demonstrates during His last days. These emotions seem to include righteous indignation, patience, enormous courage, tremendous sorrow, suffering, agony, forgiveness, and, above all, love.

I wonder if at times we misinterpret Christ's emotional life when we see Him only as a one-dimensional, nice, and happy individual. If we look to Christ as our perfect example, it appears He had access to the full range of emotions, the whole "spectrum of colors," the brilliance and depth of which we can only try to comprehend. He actually felt every emotion ever experienced by humankind during His lifetime, including all of the emotions that we will experience in our lives, *and He used them for good.* And because Christ has a perfect emotional understanding, He is able to help us in our times of need—in our emotional imperfection—through the power of the Atonement.

We must remember that we are still in emotional development and will be for a long time. I think that part of our healthy psychological and spiritual development means using earthly experiences to learn how to *feel* our feelings and use them for good purposes. But we have to start with *awareness* of our emotions—all of them—and open ourselves up to the beautiful lessons they can teach us as we strive for personal and spiritual growth.

Getting Better at Feeling

Many of the most effective psychological therapies emphasize the importance of being willing to feel emotions and observe them with as little judgment as possible. Many of us, consciously or not, have developed some unhealthy habits of emotional behavior that seem natural to us but might be harmful and can be changed. For example, if you are a single mother and automatically get defensive and angry when someone speaks to you in a way that seems to assume you live in a traditional two-parent home, changing your emotional responses in such situations will require some serious effort and concentration.

Extending this example, if one of your children plays on a soccer team and another parent asks you to take your turn with a carpool, your initial feelings as a single mother might include anger, frustration, self-pity, impatience, helplessness, or some other mix of emotions. The important thing here is to practice pausing and allowing yourself to simply feel the emotions that you have and not hastily judge yourself (or the other person). To be aware of your experiences and responses to a situation without judgment is called practicing mindfulness. Recognize and acknowledge that you have these feelings; these emotions are real and legitimate but not inherently bad or good. Of course, these emotions can be shifted over time, but in order to decide how best to handle them, you first just need to let that emotional energy flow through you. Then, as guided by the Spirit, you can work on changing the way you feel in such situations and focus on learning how to use those emotions for good in the ways that you respond and interact with others.

For a more general example, most of us need to become more skillful or adept at recognizing and learning how to handle our emotions. In my clinical experience, many emotional problems arise from trying to avoid, ignore, or become numb to our emotions. Regardless of what we are feeling, if we don't like it, most of us don't really deal with it—we just want it to go away. Most of us just want to *feel* better, but maybe the focus instead should be to get *better* at *feeling*!

I believe that one very important reason to get better at *feeling* is that uncomfortable and painful emotions seem to cause the most trouble if left unattended. If we can allow ourselves to feel those emotions and start to work with them in constructive and productive ways, we will decrease the amount of pain we feel and increase the amount of pain we are willing to bear. I think there is a strong correlation between the amount of pain we are able to bear and the depth of love or joy we can feel as well. This, however, is not an invitation for us martyrs to wallow in as much pain as we can bring on ourselves in hopes that we will also feel a great amount of joy and happiness. This type of approach will usually inhibit one's ability to feel love and joy. Remember, I want us to focus on being willing and able to feel and handle our emotions as fully and as well as possible so that we might learn from them.

There are some of you out there who might be making the argument, "Well, I just don't allow myself to get angry." If you have reached this point of emotional maturity, congratulations; keep up the good work. But even the most patient women I know lose their cool once in a while. And, as mentioned previously, not allowing ourselves to feel an emotion can be problematic. This goes for any emotion. Sadness, suffering, and grief are emotions that are uncomfortable, and most of us struggle in dealing with them well. But if we simply shut off or close down our ability (and sometimes *necessity*) to engage with, live through, and learn from these kinds of emotions, we may be unintentionally causing more long-term and complex problems.

If we are just talking about the capacity to feel at all, shutting down the ability to feel one emotion means we are likely reducing the ability to feel *any* emotion. In this sense, our feelings need to be exercised much the same as our muscles, our intellect, and our spirit. (If we only want to do "easy" exercises, we likely won't get very strong.) And if we say to ourselves, "I only want to feel happiness and joy and nice comfortable feelings—I don't want to ever feel heartbroken, embarrassed, or angry," then we are likely limiting our ability to feel and are cutting ourselves off from joy and happiness.

Being Willing to Submit to Your Full Emotional Self

My sister Rebecca Overson tells the story about the birth of her second baby as a lesson in willingness and submission. Many women fear and avoid giving birth without medication because of the physical pain that is typically involved. And while the following experience may not be for every woman, Rebecca shares what she believed was a "miraculous and painless birth" as a result of her willingness to simply submit to the birthing process.

> It was in this state of mind—this intense willingness to feel what it feels like to be alive—to intently receive everything that life has to offer me—that I gave birth to our second son.

I was totally, completely willing to experience giving birth fully, unlike I had ever done before. I knew it was going to hurt, but I was willing to feel whatever it felt like. I knew I was going to reach that intense point during transition and have thoughts like "I can't do this, I'm going to die"—and I welcomed those thoughts. I didn't take them seriously. I knew they would come, and I welcomed them. I was totally open to the possibility that this could be another 15 hours of excruciating back labor.

While in labor, I surrendered to each contraction, much like one would surrender to contractions of the respiratory diaphragm when vomiting or sneezing. As I reclined against the wall of the birthing tub, I repeatedly whispered to myself, "Just feel this. Just feel what this feels like." I just observed my body in the process, doing what it knows instinctively to do. My body was shaking uncontrollably as the baby descended down the birth canal. I felt intense pressure and my midwife said, "Honey, that's the baby's head." I couldn't believe it. I reached down and sure enough, there was his wrinkly little head beginning to crown. The contractions continued and it actually felt so good to feel him moving down the birth canal. (I would say I "pushed" but it actually felt effortless, like I was being pushed.) His head was fully born in about two contractions.

I could not believe it when he was out. He was born . . . less than two hours after hard labor began. And he was 9½ pounds! (I am only 5'3"!) No tearing, no pain, just hard work and sweet relief. I sat back down in the birthing tub and clutched him to my chest. The experience was so ecstatic, so joyful, and so incredibly wonderful. The first thing I said was, "That was awesome." While the physical sensations I experienced were very intense, it was not painful. It did not hurt! It was truly transformative, and I attribute much of the wonder of the experience to my commitment to birthing mindfully and willingly, to fully experience whatever it is that is before me. (Adapted by author from Rebecca Overson, "The Gift of Giving Life," 2010, http://thegiftofgivinglife.blogspot.com/2010/02/rebecca-oversons-story.html)

I think Rebecca's story is a good metaphor for what can happen when we meet any kind of pain with willingness and submission. It just hurts *less*. You suffer less. Psychologically and emotionally speaking, you have to be open to all of life, to the full range of emotions, if you want to allow yourself to become fully emotionally developed. It has been my experience that feeling and learning from our pain makes more room for compassion and charity.

Tools for Healthy Emotional Expression

There are so many wonderful and constructive ways for dealing with and processing your emotions. Here are a few more suggestions.

Journaling

Many people find journaling therapeutic. Simply writing out what you feel and think can be extremely helpful as you empty your head onto a page and see what's really there. You can use a book and pen, a simple piece of paper, or a computer. You don't even have to keep what you journal! There are also many free online journals that can be protected with your own password. As mentioned previously, voice memos (available on some phones) are a good option for giving voice to your feelings.

Giving expression to your emotions in some way may give you a deeper and more cathartic understanding of your emotional self. Keeping a record also provides a valuable reference for you in the future and perhaps may even bless your descendants.

Connecting with Others

Friends who don't buy into your problems are wonderful to have. Don't get me wrong—it's also helpful at times to have someone who can be sincerely sympathetic and supportive when you need that kind emotional support. However, you may achieve a greater sense of emotional honesty if there are people in your life who can, without minimizing or dismissing you or your problems, simply listen and be a lantern to help illuminate your situation and talk out your feelings with you. A friend who can offer a more complete view of what might be going on in your life in a genuinely caring manner is a great treasure. It is also a great idea to practice being the kind of friend who can listen to another without adding more ammunition to the emotional arsenal.

Creative Expression

There is something magical about losing yourself in something creative, no matter what it is you like to do. That might be dancing, cooking, drawing, sewing, writing, crafting, playing an instrument, playing with children, or playing games—anything at all that requires your full creative participation. Doing something to move energy through you is an excellent tool.

Exercise and Physical Activity

When it's not motivated by a hate for your body (don't worry, we'll address that later in the book!), exercise is one of the best ways to literally put emotional energy in motion. If you are under time and resource constraints, yoga, pilates, tai chi, and other "simple" exercises can be done when you need to stay at home. It's also important to get a change of scenery; go for a walk, a jog, a bike ride, or go swimming or hiking, whatever appeals to you. And if you have the time and means, try something new! Skiing, tennis, swimming, aerobics, golf, or fly fishing are just a few of the options available; just get your body moving. Also, try getting even more out of your activities—many women use walking with friends who offer a circle of support for both exercise and communication.

Prayer

Prayer is so much more than saying what you are grateful for and then asking for what you want! Nor does prayer have to be motivated by a desire to take negative feelings away or to fix anything (though it does seem that many of our most sincere prayers are often motivated by distress and are a cry for help). Prayer can be meditative, cathartic, a pouring out of your heart and soul to Heavenly Father just for the sake of honoring the feelings you have. He is able to hear and hold all your feelings. Try a prayer of gratitude or simply share your life with Heavenly Father and let go of trying to figure everything out. Try writing out your prayers and reflecting on the desires of your heart.

Learn to really converse with your Heavenly Father in prayer. Be patient in prayer; wait and listen. Recognize and express gratitude for the emotions that you feel while praying—especially when the Spirit touches you. The gift of inspiration is incredible.

Therapy

As a therapist, I'm sure you expected that I'd add therapy to the list. My own experiences as a *client* in therapy have been life-changing and invaluable in shaping my emotional health, my relationship skills, and my career path. There are many types of services available that are flexible and affordable for anyone's schedule and resources. Also, be aware of the hesitation in our culture to "seek professional help"; I'm so glad that the negative connotation associated with phrases such as "going to counseling" are disappearing. Just as you would not hesitate to seek attention for a physical wound, the unseen pain of emotional suffering should be treated with the same sense of importance.

<u>Mindfulness Exercises</u>

Mindfulness means giving your full attention to *this* moment, allowing things to be as they are, right now as you observe them. So much stress and anxiety can come from thoughts and feelings from the past or what might happen in the future—often aspects in our lives that are beyond our control at this time. Slowing down and paying attention to "right now" allows you to identify, express, and release emotions in a healthy way.

There are several fairly simple methods of calming yourself and slowing down your emotional responses. One simple method is to stop and breathe a few times, consciously. Simply feel what it feels like to breathe. Feel the air in your nose or in your mouth. Turn your mind's attention inward to your body, and feel what's happening. Feel your feet on the ground, feel your hands in your lap or at your side, feel your rib cage expand and your belly move with each breath. Just stop, breathe, and check in for the sake of being here, now.

Sharing Emotions in Relationships: Intimacy as "Into Me, See"

Being aware of your internal experiences and developing healthy emotional management tools are helpful for preventing burnout, but these tools are also an important part of developing healthy relationships. Sharing your honest feelings in meaningful and powerful ways with others, in word and action, plays a large part in the development of healthy intimacy and connection with other people.

Consider that intimacy means "into me, see," like a request: "Will you see into me?" The longing of every heart is to be seen, to be understood, to be cherished, to have emotional needs responded to in loving ways, and to be accepted. The ability to share your honest emotions, both joy and the pain, paves the way for true intimacy in all relationships. Developing skills to share what's in your heart with another person is one of the most important skills you can develop in life. Expressing more vulnerable emotions (such as fear, longing, and sadness) in your close family relationships tends to draw others closer to you and can elicit more nurturing and gentle responses from the people that matter most.

Three Stances in Relationships

Have you ever talked to someone who always has to one-up whatever you say? Or somebody who puts herself down all the time? You can also likely think of a person who usually makes you feel good about yourself whenever you talk with her. I've noticed that people habitually assume a particular stance in relationships and communication. Just think about a time when you got upset, were offended, or felt challenged by someone. The way you responded likely reflects one of three stances: a sword, a doormat, or a lantern.

<u>Take This Quiz!</u>

Try this: Read the following example and choose which answer most accurately reflects the way you would most likely respond in this situation. (Don't think about how you think you *should* respond—just be honest with yourself about how you actually *do* respond in a situation like this.)

Your friend Amy agrees to help you throw a baby shower for a mutual friend, Melissa. You are counting on Amy's help, but she doesn't return your phone calls or e-mails. Finally, the morning of the shower, after you've done all the work yourself, she calls and half-apologetically asks what you need. Which best describes your honest reaction?

A) "Wow. Two hours before the party starts, you're *finally* getting back to me? Well, lucky for you I did it all myself. Next time don't even bother to offer help if you aren't going to follow through."

B) "Oh, it's no big deal, I'm good. See you soon?"

C) "Amy, I am disappointed and upset that you haven't contacted me sooner. I really could have used the help that you offered. It's been frustrating not being able to get hold of you. But I'd appreciate it if you could pick up a bag of ice on your way over. Thank you."

If answer B most closely reflects your response, you are assuming a doormat stance. If answer A most closely reflects your response, you are assuming a sword stance. If answer C most closely reflects your response, you are assuming a lantern stance. There are times when you might have a "mixed" stance, but these three simple categories are very useful in describing most response styles.

<u>The Doormat</u>

Those who assume the stance of *doormat* might have a hard time identifying their emotions because they place so little value on their own feelings and opinions. They might not speak up for themselves, they might become submissive, and they might possibly be a bit childish. They often feel like they are being run over by others, they feel little internal power, and they don't feel respected by those they care about most.

One of the problems with this stance is that while others might assume you are "fine" because you don't assert your opinion, you might actually be building up resentment as you internalize frustration at not having said what you really wanted to say. Another problem that often results from this stance is discouragement or some form of depression. When we feel discounted or devalued by others, we tend to struggle with fostering our range of positive emotions.

The Sword

Those who use a *sword* stance are emotionally on guard and are likely to lash out at others when they sense even the slightest amount of danger or threat. Their weapon is drawn and they are on emotional high alert, ready to react and fight. It is both aggressive and passive-aggressive; the passive-aggressive stance is a good example of a mixed stance where you may play the part of the doormat in an initial confrontation but then passively "attack" by vowing never to trust that person again.

Doormats who get fed up with not being heard and not getting their needs met often flip into sword stance to defend themselves and their right to have a voice. Someone who assumes the sword stance might let emotions build up and then explode with cutting words or snide remarks; they might also throw up defensive walls and become cold, aloof, and unavailable. One of the most common characteristics of the sword stance is sarcasm. People get away with sarcasm because it can be funny at the time and it might be brushed aside by stating, "I was only joking." The insidious side of sarcasm is that it cuts away at other people in small slices that can eventually leave large scars. Another less directly confrontational aspect of the sword stance is gossip; unfortunately, we all know how hurtful this can be to our emotional lives.

The Lantern

In contrast, those who take the *lantern* stance have their emotional feet securely planted on the ground and are difficult to knock over. Much like a hurricane lantern, their light remains steady and strong even in the midst of a tempest. There is a calmness about them as they hold up a metaphorical light to notice what's going on in any given situation and as they make fair-minded assessments without hasty or unwarranted judgments. They aren't reactive like swords or passive like doormats. When they do get upset, they don't ignore it but deal with it as a tool for further understanding themselves and others. Being a lantern is a difficult stance and requires some refueling and maintenance. This is a good example of the need to take care of one's self in order to take care of others. A well-maintained lantern is ready and able to shine when others need it the most.

Whenever we're communicating, we are usually playing one of these three roles. I have decorative lanterns at work and at home because it reminds me that I want to stand up straight and hold up a light. I don't want to be a doormat where I just lie down while people do and say whatever they want. I don't want to be a sword where I'm being defensive, making excuses for forgetting to do something I promised to do, or making underhanded comments. I want to stand up straight, face the other person, and hold up a light.

One way to be a lantern is by clearly expressing how you are feeling and doing it without entitlement, accusation, or blame.

This is a great example from a workshop participant about how she was able to move from being a doormat to a lantern:

> When I was much younger, I felt extremely down about myself. I let the horrible things my friends were saying to me get into my thoughts. I felt alone and unloved. One day I wrote about it in my journal, and while I was in school the next day my mom read it. She was so upset from what she read that she ripped the page out of my journal, and when I got home she told me that I was selfish for not being grateful for what I did have. That experience really hurt me; I didn't feel that I was being selfish. I just felt down.
>
> From that moment on, I always kept my negative feelings buried inside me. It's been really hard for me to express my feelings over the years, and when you talked about doing what's in your best interest while at the same time being sensitive to others, it really hit me. Expressing my feelings is not being selfish. It truly felt like a weight had been lifted off my shoulders. I was shocked how free I felt.
>
> The next morning, I actually called my mom up and talked to her about that experience that we shared when I was younger. She didn't even remember it and said that she was so sorry she had done that. She said that she made many mistakes as a mother and she probably was just so frustrated with not knowing how to help me more when she felt she was doing everything she could to show me love. It was really a wonderful experience to have with my mom. We shared our deep feelings, and it truly meant the world to me.

When you have something difficult to communicate, think about which stance you automatically assume and consider how you can hold up a lantern to illuminate the situation. Being a lantern does not mean you have to prove anything or be better; that's the sword. A lantern just sheds light on life, and that's what honest and clear communication can do. Other people might not like what they see and they might not see things the way we do, but more information is available to everyone when we are standing in the light.

Pause and Reflect: Assertive Communication Tool

Here's one of my favorite tools that simplifies emotional expression, making it easier to share your feelings in a way that is more likely to be heard and understood by another. I actually use this tool with my own family all the time. Think of a situation that is bothering you right now. Maybe your spouse seems to ignore you when you talk, or your neighbor's dog keeps "fertilizing" your lawn, or your sister keeps complaining to you about her marriage but won't do anything to improve her situation.

List three of your own concerns. We'll do another exercise that centers on these concerns, so give it some thought before you write them down!

1) _____

2) _____

3) _____

Now try this: Can you articulate your problem more clearly by formatting it to fit into this sentence?

I feel _____(your emotion)

when you _____(another's specific behavior)

because I think _____ (your thought).

Here are a few examples:
- I feel sad when you come home from work and turn on the TV because I think I'm not important to you.
- I feel hurt when you come home and don't do your share of the housework because I think you are not pulling your weight.
- I feel mad when you leave your backpack and jacket on the floor because I think you don't care about your belongings.
- I feel sad when you don't include me in Girls' Night Out because I think I'm not important to you.

You can use this sentence to effectively share any kind of emotion or thought in your relationships. Try it with the three concerns you listed above, and be as specific as possible.

1) I feel _____

when you _____

because I think _____.

2) I feel _____

when you _____

because I think _____.

3) I feel _____

when you _____

because I think _____.

Sharing Emotions: How Much and How Often?

Deciding where and when to share your feelings depends on the level of closeness and commitment in the relationship. It's not helpful to overwhelm others by constantly sharing all your feelings. Being able to tolerate and soothe your own feelings internally is an important skill to develop. If a difficult emotion doesn't seem to go away, that's a signal that sharing with another trusted person might be helpful.

I find it useful to think of relationships in terms of concentric circles. At the center of the circle is Heavenly Father; He already knows your heart and wants you to pray to Him. The "inner-circle" would necessarily include Jesus Christ, as we pray to the Father in His name; as we draw on the power of the Atonement for inner strength; and as we draw on the power of the Holy Ghost to guide, comfort, and inspire us. The rule of thumb for sharing emotions is this: The closer a person is to your "inner circle," the deeper and more frequent you should be able to share your emotions with them.

Sharing specific information about your emotions is more powerful than talking in generalities. It's a more direct way of getting your needs met and peacefully communicating otherwise difficult emotions. For example, instead of lashing out with "You just aren't there for me!" try, "I feel sad when I ask if we can talk about our relationship and you say no because I think I'm not important to you." Being responsible for your feelings as you share them with others opens up opportunities for meaningful communication.

Although this formula for communicating emotions is merely a tool, not a panacea, it should help you calmly and effectively express what's going on for *you* and separate your emotional energy from your feelings so resentment doesn't fester.

This may be a good place to talk about silence and patience. Far too often we are so worried about what we want to say next (especially in heated exchanges) that we don't stop to listen or stop to think about what we're saying and how we are saying it (the *how* can be almost as important as the *what*). Avoid interrupting the other person while he or she tries to express feelings. If the other person interrupts you, ask him or her to kindly let you finish what you have to say. And be okay with some pauses and silence during a conversation.

I have a friend who likes to think carefully about what he says and how he wants to say it; this often frustrates his family and friends. Patience is truly a virtue in many aspects of our lives, especially in interpersonal communication.

One more thing to mention: as a rule-of-thumb, avoid walking out on a conversation (storming out of the room can be as symbolically violent as any other "sword" stance). The exception to this rule, however, is that if a conversation escalates to the point of being non-productive or worse, it may be better to separate for a minute (or thirty); step outside and get a breath of fresh air.

There is another kind of emotion that this model can help you express: *I feel happy when you touch my hand because I think you care about me. Thanks for doing that.* Specific feedback, whether negative or positive, is always more meaningful to receive. More often than not, open, direct, and honest communication will help you make direct requests of people or ask them to do something differently. It will also help *others* understand you.

Making Requests of Others

The second part of identifying and sharing how you feel is to determine whether you would like to make a specific request.

If you consider the examples you used in the previous exercise, it might appear as an opportunity to dump your emotions on others. No! If you look again, you'll notice that the statement of how you feel often needs to be followed up with a specific request. Sometimes we expect the people in our lives to automatically know what we want, and we get upset that they don't give it to us. For example, if you get your hair done and nobody says anything, you feel as though nobody cares. A temptation would be to throw out a complaint such as "Well, you don't care about me anyway" and leave it at that. If you want to prevent emotional burnout, you need to ask for what you want (without being overly sensitive) and do it in a clear and loving way.

If you struggle with asking for what you want, try beginning with the phrase *"It would mean a lot to me if . . ."* For example:

—I feel sad when you come home from work and turn on the TV because I think I'm not important to you. *It would mean a lot to me if* you would come home, give me a hug, sit down and talk to me for twenty minutes before you turn on the TV.

—I feel hurt when you come home and don't do your share because I think you are not pulling your weight. *It would mean a lot to me if* you would come home and ask if I need help with anything.

—I feel mad when you leave your backpack and jacket on the floor because I think you don't care about my efforts to keep the house clean. *It would mean a lot to me if* you would put your things where they belong.

—I feel sad when you don't include me in Girls' Night Out because I think I'm not important to you. *It would mean a lot to me if* you would extend an invitation to me next time.

If and how the other person decides to honor your request is entirely up to him or her. But if something really bothers you, it is in your court to a) identify what you are feeling, b) express it clearly and in a non-threatening way, and c) ask clearly and calmly for what you want. You don't have to be apologetic or full of pity. Simply offer your truth regarding what you feel, what you think, and what would mean a lot to you. It is an exercise in standing up and shining your own light instead of feeling trampled on and unimportant or always having your emotional "sword" at-the-ready.

Pause and Reflect: It Would Mean a Lot to Me If . . .

Using the three concerns you listed above, identify what your requests are in each situation.

1. It would mean a lot to me if _____

_____

_____

2. It would mean a lot to me if _____

_____

_____

3. It would mean a lot to me if _____

_____

_____

Finding healthy ways to process your emotions is front-line prevention for emotional burnout. Learning how to share emotions in your relationships is the foundation for true intimacy and long-term mutual fulfillment.

CURE 2: GIVE YOURSELF PERMISSION TO SAY AN INSPIRED "NO"

Why We Over-Commit

I'M CONVINCED THAT MANY WOMEN are burned out because they don't know how to say no when doing so would be appropriate and honest. Taking on more commitments than you can handle will leave you feeling overwhelmed. You know the scripture that admonishes us to not run faster than we have strength? In both the Church and in life you will be presented with endless opportunities to serve and give. I really mean *endless*. You cannot and will not be able to say yes to them all; doing so will result in exhaustion and emotional burnout.

Saying no is an important skill.

> Myth: I should always say yes to reasonable requests.
>
> Truth: You have human limitations. Saying no is an important boundary for self-care and is crucial to preventing burnout.

Just ask anyone in a visible leadership position like a PTA president, bishop, Relief Society president, stake president, or other Church and community leaders. All kinds of opportunities are requested of them, more than they could ever handle. They have to become adept at figuring out which they are able say yes to and which they cannot. Yet saying no to anything that falls into the enormous general category of what would be "helpful"—even something you *should* say no to—can be a bit scary for most of us. This goes not only for direct requests, but also indirect opportunities to volunteer when a sign-up sheet is passed around. Think for a moment about the last time you said yes when you wanted to say no. What about saying no made you so afraid?

I suspect, just from my experience, that saying no is a challenge for women in general because many of us instinctively or culturally feel a desire to be full of charity and take care of others. The LDS culture, with an expectation to serve coupled with our commitment to take care of others, may magnify our reluctance to say no. More than anything we are trying to be Christ-like, do good works, be anxiously engaged in a good cause, and serve others. At times we may not feel able to say no because we are afraid of offending or disappointing someone. I want to pause and reiterate an important doctrinal point: The power of the Atonement can, when needed, give us strength to carry us beyond our normal capacity to serve. In his April 2012 general conference address, President Henry B. Eyring bore powerful witness of the Lord's willingness to support us through our deepest trials—even assuring us that we are never alone in the Lord's service and that He has promised angels on our right and our left to bear us up (see Henry B. Eyring, "Mountains to Climb," *Ensign*, May 2012).

Survey: Can You Say No?

57 percent of women surveyed feel they take on more commitments than they can handle.

74 percent of women surveyed have difficulty saying no when asked to do something they don't want to do.

However, when we couple all of the innumerable, often unseen acts of goodness that we do of our own free will with all that we are expected and asked to do that stretch us to and beyond our limits, our hours and days may begin to seem overwhelming. When righteous desires begin to feel like a heavy obligation, it can be hard to feel the energy or inspiration required to serve others.

I really believe that an important skill in preventing emotional burnout is the ability to say no. So many women I counsel are absolutely paralyzed with fear when it comes to saying no to *anything!* For example, what if you're trying to cut back on sweets and your visiting teacher offers you a freshly baked cookie. You want to say no, but the cookie looks so good . . . and you don't want to offend her. Or perhaps your brother asks to borrow money from you during a time when money is tight for you too. You want to say no, but you say yes out of guilt and obligation. What is going on here?

I can't help but notice how masterful my children are at saying no to my requests. I have four children: two boys and two girls. When my youngest daughter was two, guess what her first sentence was? "No, Mommy." She said it a hundred times a day, without hesitation. During my oldest daughter's teenage years, she appeared to have no problem saying, "No, I don't want to!"

Yet somehow as we grow up and become women, we get the idea that it's not okay to say no—*ever*—or maybe we just forget how to say no.

Learning to say no doesn't mean saying no all the time. To be clear, I am *not* implying that you start saying no to *everything*. What I am suggesting is that some of us can actually love and serve more effectively when we feel we have the *option* of saying no to the things in life that are of less importance in the context of obligations and priorities in our lives at the time. Saying no is sometimes just as appropriate as saying yes. It's not a swear word. When you say no from an honest and heartfelt place, it lets people know what they can or can't count on from you.

One way to ease into saying no when appropriate is to practice saying one of the following phrases: "let me think about that," and "let me get back to you." These simple phrases will give you some

Workshop Comments: Why I Can't Say No

In my therapy office and in my workshops, I hear these common reasons women have difficulty saying no:
—I don't want to disappoint others.
—I should be able to do it all.
—I'm afraid to say no because people will think less of me.
—I want to help.
—If I say no, I'll feel guilty.
—I want to please others.
—I feel pressured by others.
—If I say no, people will stop asking me.
—If they ask me, it must be important to them.
—If I don't do it, no one else will.
—If I can't do it all, it means I am weak, unwilling, or not good enough.
—I don't want to add to another person's burden.
—I don't want other people to say no to me when I ask them for something.
—I feel I owe it to some people to always say yes because they have done so much for me.
—I want to be generous and giving, and saying no feels selfish.
—I feel I should do as much good as possible to make up for my faults and shortcomings.

much-needed time to pause and reflect on what needs to take priority, how much you have on your schedule, and how much of yourself you have to give.

Being honest about a no can also spare you lingering feelings of guilt or "not being good enough." It's really about being honest in your dealings with other people as guided and prompted by divine inspiration.

Pause and Reflect: Saying No

In what situations do I have difficulty saying no when I know I should?

_____

_____

_____

_____

If I say no, I'm afraid that:

_____

_____

_____

_____

If I say no, it means that . . .

_____

_____

_____

_____

What messages did I hear or learn from my early experiences about saying no?

_____

_____

_____

_____

How did my parents respond when I said no to them as a child or teen?

_____

_____

_____

_____

How do I feel when I say yes when I really want to say no?

_____

_____

_____

_____

The concept of giving yourself permission to say no and putting yourself first may seemingly contradict what you've been taught about the importance of serving others and putting them first. The focus of this book is teaching you the ability to serve others more effectively by sufficiently maintaining your well-being. So let's examine the connection between the concepts of service and self-care more closely.

Service and Self-Care: Losing Yourself and Finding Yourself

"Whosoever shall seek to save his life shall lose it; and whosoever shall lose his life shall preserve it" (Luke 17:33). How does this seemingly illogical statement from the scriptures have helpful meaning for our purposes here? Many may look to this scripture as a mandate to ignore or neglect themselves—and, to be clear, a sense of forgetting yourself and focusing on the needs of others that *can* be valuable. However, in my experience I find that this type of application can tend to get turned into a default attitude of an "others always come before me" approach to life.

> Myth: I have to lose myself completely to find myself.
> Truth: I must take good care of myself so there is more of me to give as I lose myself in service of others.

It's important to find healthier ways of approaching this paradox. In certain contexts, "losing your life" can also mean letting go of old, unrighteous ways. As I've pondered this scripture, I've realized that it's not an *either/or* problem—it's not saying you have to choose to live *only* for others or *only* for yourself. President Gordon B. Hinckley said, "In other words, he who lives *only* unto himself withers and dies, while he who forgets himself in the service of others grows and blossoms in this life and in eternity" (Gordon B. Hinckley, "Whosoever Will Save His Life," *Ensign*, August 1982, 3; emphasis added). As I understand it, if we live *only unto ourselves* we will "wither and die," but that doesn't appear to mean that we should entirely leave ourselves out of the equation and completely neglect our own needs. Losing yourself in the service of others and not including yourself at all often leads to losing yourself *period* and doing so at the *expense* of those you love.

Elder M. Russell Ballard emphasized the importance of self-care when he said that those who don't take time to replenish themselves eventually find that they are drawing from an empty well and don't have what they need to give others—even their own children (see M. Russell Ballard, "Daughters of God," *Ensign*, May 2008, 110). It's important to set aside time and energy for the things that "replenish" you and give you water to fill your empty well.

A very wise client taught me a profound lesson about the scriptural meaning of losing yourself in the service of others. She suggested that this scripture in Luke could also mean that we lose our *carnal* self in service of others, not lose our entire *identity*. In other words, perhaps the goal is to lose your false (worldly, natural, temporal) self in order to discover your true (spiritual, eternal) self. You matter to God, others, and yourself. "Losing your life" doesn't mean that you and your needs—emotional, spiritual, physical, and relationship needs—don't matter. On the contrary, Heavenly Father needs spiritual, strong, passionate, skilled, and emotionally developed women to be lights in the darkness of a fallen world.

In commenting about the strength of LDS women, Elder Quentin L. Cook said that LDS women are not incredible because they somehow manage to escape the difficulties of life—lack of opportunities, problems with marriage, sorrow through the choices of their children, struggles with their health—but because they confront those difficulties and, through it all, maintain their strength and stay committed to their faith. He has observed that in addition to meeting their own difficulties, LDS women consistently lift up others who face their own struggles (see Quentin L. Cook, "LDS Women Are Incredible!" *Ensign*, May 2011, 19–20).

I think this statement gives great insight into how women can be more effective in leading Christ-like lives. While it is true that we have mortal and earthly limitations, we can and should look to the life of Christ as the perfect example of service. From my perspective as a therapist, Christ is our example of what it looks like to have a strong sense of self. As I see it and as far as I can comprehend it, He was self-actualized, fully developed, and transcended the things of this world. He had mastery over the carnal self, and His motives were purely based on His love for God and clarity of purpose.

As we strive to be as Christ-like as we can in the service of others, we must acknowledge that we are human, fallible, and prone to stumble. As we occasionally (or frequently, as the case may be) falter in our attempts to be filled with the perfect love of charity, we must remember that we, as individuals of infinite worth ourselves, need to care for ourselves as well. I have seen too many good women in my therapy practice who have spent years fervently serving and busily putting others first in a futile attempt to fill a growing emotional and spiritual emptiness inside. Giving everything we have without replenishing ourselves just doesn't work; too many of us end up feeling weak and exhausted instead.

Well-Being in Losing Yourself for His Sake

"He that findeth his life shall lose it: and he that loseth his life for my sake shall find it" (Matt. 10:39). I have often asked myself a difficult and honest question—a soul-searching question—about this scripture: *How is it possible to find a sense of well-being while losing myself in the service of others?* In a state of exhaustion, one of my clients poured her heart out to her Father in sincere prayer, asking, "How much is enough?"—meaning, how much can and should we give? The answer came after much pondering, counseling, and prayer: We must give all that we can—not for our own or for other's sake, but for the Lord's sake. We give all that we can *according to the will of the Lord*.

What is losing ourselves "for [His] sake"? Perhaps it means operating in life with a greater sense of eternal purpose. It might also describe living with the awareness that we are fulfilling our mission, following the Spirit, and becoming instruments in God's hands. It likely means acknowledging and increasing the gifts God has given us. It's probably a lot of other things too, but sometimes we seem to have forgotten the part about "for *my* sake." For *whom*, exactly, are we doing all of this "losing of our lives"? We are doing it for our God; we are on the Lord's errand. Many of us are running around busily losing ourselves, but we are not losing ourselves for *His* sake. If we are simply ignoring ourselves, putting ourselves last, forgetting that we matter, we will feel lost.

I've worked with a lot of busy people who haven't found themselves yet. They're just lost, because they're not losing themselves for *His sake.*

Jane, an exhausted mother of four children, came to me for therapy after discovering her husband had a pornography problem. His sexual issues brought to the surface her own unresolved feelings of shame and worthlessness. As a survivor of childhood sexual abuse, Jana had never told her parents what had happened to her and had kept her "secret" for decades. Living by the false assumption that if she ignored her abuse it would fade away, Jane learned to manage her shame, frustration, and anger by overcompensating. She poured her heart and energy into family life and Church service. She believed that if she could just be selfless enough, serve diligently, be an amazingly supportive wife, and be a dedicated mother, somehow she would finally feel worthy of love and feel "good" enough. She had hoped that by losing herself she might find her family and the good life she had always wanted for herself.

Jane came to me because her faulty equation wasn't producing the result for which she'd hoped. She was losing herself in service but hadn't found herself. Together we worked to explore what her true source of worth was and what the Lord wanted for her. She came to realize that ultimately she had to be spiritually and emotionally strong and grounded to find herself. She had to lose herself in the service of others—especially her family—according to the will of the Lord while constantly nourishing her body, mind, heart, and soul.

We Are Stewards of Our Emotional Energy

Deciding where we invest our time and energy is part of our stewardship in life. Because of our agency we get to decide where we are going to invest what we have been given. We are the ones who get to choose what is more important to us and when. It's our choice, and the goal is to have the Spirit with us to help us make the choices that the Lord would want us to make.

I like to use the following analogy: Your life is like a platter of fruit and vegetables, and your goal is to eat healthy. But if you pile everything on it (even *only* good things), what happens? You can only pile so much onto the platter before it is filled and things start falling off. In my experience the things that start falling off are the most important things when I'm overcommitted: personal scripture study, meaningful prayer, family home evening. Those are some of the first things to go, and I and consequently my loved ones always pay a price for it. And that shouldn't be the way we manage our lives.

No One Ever Died from Disappointment

I spent many years being fearful of disappointing others, even people I'd never met. I wanted everyone to like me. Over the years I've learned that people aren't as fragile as we think they are. No one ever died from being disappointed. Being able to say no has been a really important skill for me in keeping my priorities straight and sparing myself the guilty feelings that come from failing to do or be everything that everyone else wants (or what I *think* everyone else wants). For example, I've gotten good at graciously saying no to speaking and singing invitations unless it sounds fun and energizing, works with my family's schedule, and is something that I feel prompted by the Spirit to do. It's liberating to know that giving an honest no allows me to focus on what really matters most in my life.

Your Honest "No" Can Be a Gift to Others

My older sister Carrie and I had our two oldest children around the same time. Each of us had a boy first and then a girl, so it was really great when they were little and played a lot together. One day, a long time ago, I called her and said, "Hey, can Tanner and Madeline come over and play today with Christian and Beatrice?"

She said, "No, that just sounds too hard today." (Luckily I had five other sisters to call!)

My point is that she could have said "yes" out of a sense of obligation, a sincere desire to help, just plain old guilt, or a combination of these feelings. But her honest "no" was a gift to me because it gave me a clear picture of her reality instead of a false sense of security (it also gave me a healthy example from which to learn). That day she was not in a position to give my children the attention they needed, and that was good to know so I could find another resource for help at that time.

If you have ever been in any kind of organizational leadership position, you know you would rather have people tell you no right from the start than have them say yes to something and not do it well or not do it at all—that kind of dishonesty does not serve anyone well. It's extremely stressful to discover something is not taken care of when you were told that it would be. Everyone would rather have the truth so they know where they stand and what needs to be done from there.

A Dishonest "Yes" Breeds Resentment

One of our core values as Latter-day Saints is being honest and having integrity. Have you ever considered that it is dishonest to say "yes" when you really mean "no"? It's so tricky—we want to please, and we want to help; we want to do our share, and we want to do what's right. But I know from my own experience there are times when I really wish I felt free to say no and feel at peace about it, yet I found myself saying yes. I have seen a dishonest "yes" create distance, stress, resentment, and guilt. One cute older woman in a workshop in California told me, "My definition of stress is when your gut says no and your mouth says, 'Certainly!'"

Perhaps it is the dishonest "yes" to too many things (even if they're all good things) that contributes to a hectic life. When we are dishonest with ourselves we are likely to end up harboring feelings of resentment; this state of emotional being can make it very difficult to feel the Spirit.

The Savior's perfect life beautifully illustrates the clarity of purpose and priority. Elder Neal A. Maxwell said, "As far as I can see, Jesus was never hectically involved. This is all the more marvelous when we realize that so much of His mortal Messiahship was crowded into only three very busy years" (Neal A. Maxwell, "Wisdom and Order," *Ensign*, June 1994, 43).

In my late teens, I started writing and recording music and doing concerts and performances. I had the hardest time saying no to requests. I wanted to please everyone, so I would automatically think, *How can I make it work?* I'd go to great lengths to rearrange everything in my life to cram in all my commitments. After a while I realized that trying to say yes to every event request wasn't working for me. Did I really think I was the only person on earth

a musical number? I realized that the whole world didn't revolve
~~~~~ that if I said no, the youth conference would go on, the fireside
would go on. I have had to learn to be okay with saying no—without guilt—when
I have been inspired to say no, even to good things I wanted to do.

Why an Inspired "No" Is Important

There are several reasons why I feel the ability to say an inspired "no" is
important. It can help set boundaries for ourselves, helps us recognize our
limitations and abilities, helps to prevent emotional burnout, helps us identify our needs (which can help fortify our gifts), and helps expand our expression of having a self.

"No" Sets an Important Boundary

"No" shows that while you belong to families, neighborhoods, communities, and the Church, you are an individual person with your own thoughts,
feelings, and desires. Saying "no" (just as saying "yes") to certain things acknowledges that you are unique and that your voice does matter. For many
of us who have assumed the doormat stance for as long as we can remember,
being able to say "no" is a critical part of being able to develop a healthy sense
of self; it helps us be more sincere and genuine when we say "yes."

"No" Means Acceptance of Your Limitations

Many of us live as though we are omnipotent, omniscient, and omnipresent
in this life! We think we can be everything to everyone and be everywhere all of
the time. You are a human being with human limits. Saying "no" is a way of acknowledging that you have mortal limitations. It forces you to prioritize your life
as inspired, based on what is most important to attend to right now. Learning this,
in turn, helps you come to know your abilities and true potential.

"No" Prevents Burnout!

Saying no and setting limits allows you to avoid feeling overwhelmed and
becoming overcommitted. Saying no with honesty frees you from guilt and
resentment. You have to pick and choose where to invest your time, energy,
and other resources; exercising prayer, you can learn to do this in an inspired
way. One workshop participant once commented, "When I say 'no' I'm saying 'yes' to something more important."

"No" Helps You Identify Your Needs

If you are someone who struggles to know what you want for yourself, you
can use "no" to help identify your needs more clearly. Often, I help clients figure

out what they want to do by eliminating the "definitely nots" from their options. I recently worked with a woman whose children are all in school. She had a desire to expand her talent and passion for cooking and entertaining into a paying job. But she was paralyzed by not knowing exactly what she wanted to do. I encouraged her to pick one option to focus on and then told her to give herself permission to change her mind at any time by saying, "No, this isn't what I want to do," and then try something else.

"No" Is an Expression of Having a Self

It is important for your psychological and spiritual well-being to realize that you are you. Being able to think for yourself and express your desires is exercising God's all-important gift of agency.

Strategies for Saying an Inspired "No"

Seek Guidance from the Spirit

Ask for guidance from the Spirit about what you should and shouldn't do. Ponder it, pray about it, and counsel with your Church leaders when you need to. There may be times you have an assurance from the Spirit that you should say yes to something even though you want to say no, and vice versa. Follow the Spirit.

Ask God to Order Your Day

One workshop participant said, "I ask God to order my day. God has called me to minister to my neighborhood and to take care of my sons. I try to seek what the Lord would have me do so I don't feel overwhelmed. When I have confirmation that God wants me to do something, then the stress dissipates. I have to do only what He wants, not what everyone else wants."

I just love that. Let His priorities be your priorities.

Take Time to Think about It

Take time to think things over. When someone asks something of you, it's okay to say, "Let me get back to you." That is one of the best phrases ever. Take the time you need in order to make the decision. You may look at your calendar and realize, *You know what? I have a commitment for a quiet house that hour. I am not available.* It's your decision how to spend your time. But if you say that you will get back to someone, remember that you actually *do* need to get back to that person! Don't just avoid it, or you'll add another unfinished thing to your list! Try it: *Let me get back to you.*

Remember That It Is, in Fact, Your Decision

Remind yourself that the decision *really* is up to you. It's your decision! You may have controlling people in your life who want to decide where you're going to spend your time and what you are or aren't going to do. And there are others who are masters at manipulation or at sending people on guilt trips. Continually remind yourself that it is your time and your decision, not theirs.

Remember That "No" Can Be Honorable

No can be just as valid and reassuring as yes can be. You don't have to hang your head in shame because you can't do everything people expect you to do. No is an honorable response when it is delivered in love and honesty. It keeps expectations clean and clear.

Offer "No" with True Empathy

Saying no under a difficult circumstance can be easier when you use empathy. You can say, "Gosh, I can see you're really struggling, but I'm just not able to do that. I'm so sorry. Thank you for asking me. Please ask me next time." An empathetic no makes it easier, since no one wants to be uncaring or hurtful. This is especially helpful when expressed as an informed and inspired decision rather than impulsive or reactive "no."

Give a Simple "No" with No Explanation Needed

Try offering an honest no without all the reasons and justification. You don't have to get the other person to understand or agree with you. You can simply say no without owing any explanation. This is a difficult one for me to do. I feel that because someone has asked something of me, I somehow owe them an explanation of why I can't do it. However, I've noticed that sometimes, after offering my explanation, the person tries to rearrange my schedule so she can get what she wants. "If you leave your meeting ten minutes early, you'll have time to drop me off at my hair appointment and you'll only be fifteen minutes late picking up your kids from school, right?" Yikes! Sometimes the best answer is a simple no. Sometimes your response isn't informed by something as simple as the number of hours or minutes in a day; if you feel guided by the Spirit to say "no," that is sufficient.

We are counseled in the scriptures and by our Church leaders to listen to the Spirit to guide our lives. This guidance does not always come to our minds in complete logical sentences; more often than not it is a feeling (good or bad) or a "stupor of thought." Since it is awfully difficult to clearly verbalize and reasonably justify your reasons for saying "no" when you are not sure of those reasons yourself—you are only sure that you have received guidance of the Holy Ghost—I would suggest trying something such as, "That's just not going to work."

Here's an example: Your teen asks if he can drive to a party at a friend's house on Friday night. You may feel prompted that this is a bad idea for your teenager but you're not sure why. Try saying, "That's not going to work" Or "I don't feel good about that." He will likely ask, demandingly, "Well, why not?" Repeat your simple answer. Your teenager might keep pressing for a reasonably articulated answer until he realizes he is bumping into your boundary. If he simply won't settle, you'll just have to say, "I just feel like 'no' is the right answer."

If you are sure of your inspired prompting and you feel that the timing and situation is right, you might consider sharing the spiritual prompting you received— especially when the situation involves your child or someone you love. If that person been taught the gospel, he or she will likely understand—or at least accept—your seemingly simple "no." This is also a great opportunity to teach your children about listening for and following the guidance of the Holy Spirit.

Realize That Other People Also Need the Blessings of Giving Service

Sometimes we think we are being asked personally to do something when we are not. If a question is asked to a group of people, don't feel that you are personally on the spot to respond or to volunteer. You can't do everything for everyone, and if you say yes to everything, others may miss that opportunity to serve.

One workshop participant shared this experience about giving herself permission to say no:

> At times I felt like if I didn't say yes to everything that I wasn't a good member of the Church. Over time I've realized that I don't have to attend every single activity and every fireside and sign up to take dinner every time a list is passed around in Relief Society. I do it when I can. . . . I have to decide what's important, and let it be enough to just do what I can do. I know I'm making every effort [to serve], but I also have to include myself in all the serving I'm doing.

Use One of These Helpful Phrases

Here are a few more suggested phrases for offering an honest no:
"I can't give you an answer right now, will you check back with me?"
"I want to, but I'm unable to."
"I'm not able to commit to that right now."
"I really appreciate you asking me, but I can't do it."

"I understand you really need my help, but I'm just not able to say yes to that. I'm so sorry."

"I'm going to say no for now. I'll let you know if something changes."

"I'm honored that you would ask me, but my answer is no."

"No, I can't do that, but here's what I *can* do . . .

"I just don't have that to give right now."

What about Church Callings?

Inevitably when I talk in workshops about saying no, someone asks, "What about Church callings? I've been taught to never turn down a calling."

Let me be very clear. I would never suggest that anyone turn down a Church calling or an opportunity to provide meaningful service! I believe that callings are inspired and provide opportunities for growth. Yet Church leaders may not be fully aware of what you have on your plate at any given time. If you feel overwhelmed when offered a Church calling, counsel with your leader. Let him know more details about your current life situation or struggles; inspiration, for you and others, often comes with information. Counsel with the Lord and seek your confirmation that this calling is where He would have you serve at this time. Seek the guidance of the Holy Spirit. You are entitled to confirmation that this calling is for you at this time.

We all should be looking for ways to serve and help others, not for ways to get out of serving. I simply want to suggest that "no" isn't a bad word, and that it can play an important part in how you go about taking good care of yourself and your loved ones.

CURE 3: DO YOUR EMOTIONAL FAMILY HISTORY

What Is Emotional Family History?

FAMILY HISTORY IS A PRIORITY in the LDS Church and is becoming increasingly popular worldwide. It's important to research your ancestors so you can have their ordinance work performed in the temple. But it's also important to know where they—and you—come from. Besides knowing the historical facts about where your ancestors originated, it's also beneficial to know your family's health history. And here's something we don't often hear emphasized: Have you ever thought about your family's emotional and relationship history? We inherit all kinds of ideas, attitudes, patterns, and beliefs from our families in addition to physical traits and medical issues.

One of the first stages in therapy is helping people understand the impact the past has on what brought them to their current situation. Emotional family history means doing some work to uncover and understand the emotional and relational patterns inherited and/or learned from your parents and grandparents. More than likely, those patterns have been passed down to you in subtle or even not-so-subtle ways.

Emotional history generally includes two historically argued facets: nature and nurture. The things you inherited by nature are those traits to which you might have a genetic predisposition; obvious examples are physical traits, talents, and limitations. Less obvious examples include the inner intellectual, emotional, and even spiritual aspects of who you are as an eternal individual and as part of a mortal family. For example, the heritage you receive from your family might include tendencies toward depression, anxiety, and addictions. These are not deterministic traits—they are simply part of who you are, and it can help to know that.

The traits you inherited through nurture include learned patterns of how to manage emotions and how to engage in relationships. You learned these patterns by watching your caretakers and family in day-to-day interactions.

The basic assumptions and rules of relationships and emotions were often passed on to you by your parents and passed on to them by their parents, and so on. Examples of these might be things like "It's not okay to be angry" or "When there is conflict, it's best to leave the situation."

The awareness of both the nature and nurture traits and patterns that have been passed down to you allows you to understand yourself better and to be more aware of your emotional vulnerabilities. It can help you take responsibility for your emotional life. Like puzzle pieces, the more pieces you have in place, the more clearly you can see the picture of yourself, which includes all of the patterns passed down to you.

Redefining "Honoring Your Parents"

Some of my clients have expressed the fear that seeking to know their emotional family history is somehow "not honoring" their parents and grandparents. You might worry that finding out about the not-so-favorable things is dishonoring your family. I have found the opposite to be true!

It seems that the more emotional and relational puzzle pieces I put in place about my parents and grandparents, the more empathetic I am toward their struggles. So many of us tend to blame our parents for what they did or did not do "right" in our upbringing. Doing my emotional family history helps me to look at my parents with a more compassionate eye. My dad's father died at age thirty-five when my dad was ten years old. My mom had a chronically ill sister who required a lot of her parents' attention. When I look back and reflect on the struggles of my parents and imagine what it was like to be in their shoes, their behavior makes more sense to me. I have more pieces of the puzzle.

> ### Survey: Mental Health Issues in Families
>
> 74 percent of women surveyed have family members who have suffered from mental health issues.
>
> 54 percent of women surveyed have family members who have received professional counseling.

Personally, having more information about my parents' emotional history has helped me to honor them—and the same thing applies to my grandparents and other relatives. I have more appreciation for what they gave me and therefore can honor the efforts they made. I see what their struggles were, what they did to cope with those struggles, and what they've passed on to me.

I think most people want to do things better or differently than how they were raised, even if it is just a little bit better. This is especially important if you were raised in an unhealthy environment; we can ultimately "blame" our parents or ancestors for only so much. Remember, how we use our agency to live our lives is our choice. I think one of God's ways of helping us heal is to help us do a little bit better than our parents, and help our kids do a little bit better than we have done. We move toward healing, toward wholeness, one step at a time.

It *is* more work and more responsibility to know what has been passed down to you. But if you are going to somehow be affected by it, wouldn't you rather know what it is and deal with it powerfully?

Three of my four grandparents had serious heart problems. I'm glad I know the health history of my grandparents be-

---

Workshop Comments: What if My Ancestor Was . . . ?

Although the discovery of your emotional and relational family history can be very liberating, I have seen that there is sometimes a hesitancy to find out about this aspect of a family. Some reasons for this might be:
—I'm afraid I might find out something bad.
—I might find out I've inherited something I'm now stuck with.
—I'll have to own it and take responsibility for it.
—Knowing my family issues feels like it is taking away part of my agency to act for myself.
—It's more work.
—It's showing dishonor to my parents and grandparents.

---

cause it helps me know that I am likely vulnerable to heart problems. I get my cholesterol checked, and that history motivates me to get on the treadmill even when I really don't want to. Knowing my family health history may prolong my life because I'm aware of my vulnerabilities and I can actively work to remedy or address them. It's the same with emotional heritage. It can help you take care of yourself!

I want to challenge you to be a little bit more curious about what you've inherited or learned from your family emotionally, psychologically, and relationally. I'm not saying you have to spend time digging up dirt on your extended family members. That's not particularly helpful. I do think it's important to get a general sense of where you are coming from, your family's mental health history, and some of the relationship patterns you were exposed to while growing up.

Every Family Has Struggles

One of the most common things that I hear in my professional practice is that women feel so alone. When you're struggling with relationship problems, marriage problems, or depression, you do feel alone. When you have a child with an addiction, when your marriage is in crisis, or when your parent leaves the Church, it's easy to feel alone because you think you are the only one with

Myth: Struggling with emotional, mental, or relationship problems is a sign of personal or spiritual weakness.
Truths: Emotional, mental, and relationship problems are part of our earthly experience.

that issue. But you are not alone. Everyone is dealing with something—and while your problem(s) might be experienced by many women, no one is coping with the problem exactly in the same way you are coping with it. We are all in this together and have much to share that can strengthen us.

It's okay. We are human. Our human experience includes trials. My extended family has dealt with substance abuse, teen pregnancy, depression, anxiety, divorce, suicide—pretty much everything. So much for being a "perfect family"! Knowing that we all struggle at least tells us we are all in the same boat. When you look at your neighbor and think, "She has it all together," please realize that you don't know what's really going on inside her life. Nobody has it all together. We all live in a fallen world, we all have physical bodies, and we're all trying to figure out how everything works and how to do the best with what we were given.

Survey: Main Reasons Family Members Went to Counseling

1. Depression
2. Marriage problems
3. Anxiety
4. Substance Abuse
5. Abuse
6. Family/Child Issues
7. Eating Disorder
8. Self-esteem
9. Addiction
10. Anger and Grief (tied)

Pause and Reflect: Your Family Struggles

Which mental or emotional health issues have any of your family members struggled with?

_____

_____

_____

_____

This Life *Is* the Preparation

Several years ago, just after my parents divorced, I became acutely aware of the problems with which my family of origin was struggling. The end of my parents' marriage prompted me to question my own life decisions. I vented to a wise, older female friend about how unprepared I felt for what life was giving me and that it seemed unfair.

I said to her, "We do a horrible job preparing our children for major, life-altering decisions, don't we? I mean, how am I supposed to know how to get through this mortal mess?"

(Think about this: How do you know when you're ready to get married? Well, you get married—then you find out you're either ready or you're not. How do you know when you're ready to be a parent? When you have a child! You get ready—you learn to cope really fast because you have no other choice.)

I then told her, "I just don't get this. Life seems like a setup for failure."

She looked at me and she said, "Julie, this life *is* the preparation." That *really* changed my perspective.

I thought, *You mean I don't have to have everything figured out right now? I can stumble?* Wow! It's *okay* that my family isn't without flaws because we're *preparing* to be an eternal family. We're working at it the only way we can—by actually doing it now—but we are not there yet. This *is* the preparation. This is the preparation of how to manage a body and how to manage relationships and how to manage emotions. We're not going to do it perfectly yet because we don't know how. We are still practicing.

What a huge relief it was to let myself and everybody else off the gotta-be-perfect here-and-now hook. My mom had a magnet on her refrigerator that said, "Nobody has it all together. That's like trying to eat once and for all." We are not "finished" yet.

Pause and Reflect: Childhood Messages

Think about the comments and messages you received as a child. Don't be concerned whether the message was true or false, just if it was frequently repeated or implied. What messages did you receive about:

Your intelligence:

_____

_____

_____

_____

Your role in your family:

_____

_____

_____

_____

Your feelings:

_____

_____

_____

_____

The value of education:

_____

_____

_____

_____

What you'd do when you grew up:

_____

_____

_____

_____

Money:

_____

_____

_____

_____

Parenting:

_____

_____

_____

_____

Religion/spirituality:

_____

_____

_____

_____

Feminine behavior:

_____

_____

_____

_____

Masculine behavior:

_____

_____

_____

_____

Your appearance:

_____

_____

_____

_____

Your emotions:

_____

_____

_____

_____

Now ask yourself:

How do these messages affect what I'm doing in my life?

_____

_____

_____

_____

What impacts me in a positive way?

_____

_____

_____

What impacts me in a negative way?

_____

_____

_____

_____

Your answers to the previous exercise should increase your curiosity and consciousness about your emotional family history. As you read through your answers, try not to *judge* yourself, your parents, your grandparents, or other influential people in your life—instead, use the information to *make sense* of your current struggles. Keep in mind that each of us grew up in different families with different beliefs of what family is, what men do, what women do, what marriage is, who is responsible for what, how to parent, and so forth. If we go through life not conscious of any of that, we may repeat things that we don't want to repeat.

Consider living your life based on conclusions your grandparents drew. Their conclusions may or may not be relevant to your life. But if you are aware of the patterns that are running your life, you can choose to either keep them or let them go in order to make room for something more authentic for you. Which brings us to another reason we tend to avoid looking at our emotional family history: Being conscious of it means you have to do something about it. The good news of the gospel is that, through the power of the Atonement and the guidance of the Spirit, you have the power and influence to head in the direction you want your life to go instead of repeating your family's patterns.

Pause and Reflect: Having Empathy for Parents

List any issues you know or suspect your parents struggled with.

Look at your answers from the Childhood Messages exercise above. What do you think your parents were going through emotionally or relationally that may have contributed to messages they passed on to you?

How does this help you understand your emotional family history?

There Are No Perfect Families

The first words in the Book of Mormon are, "I, Nephi, having been born of *goodly* parents . . ." (1 Ne. 1:1). I remind myself that Nephi didn't say he had *perfect* parents. His father Lehi was a prophet who had both righteous and rebellious children. The rebellious acts of Laman and Lemuel didn't mean Lehi wasn't a good prophet or father. In that same verse, Nephi states he was taught by his father, and had seen "many afflictions in the course of my days" and yet he was "highly favored of the Lord." Nephi experienced pain *while* at the same time being favored by God. I wonder if we add to our pain by thinking we should be perfect parents, or that having wayward children means we are doing something wrong. Nephi experienced afflictions and was highly favored.

It's stressful to think that our families are supposed to be perfect and that all of our children should stay close to the Gospel and do everything we think they are

Myth: If I'm righteous enough, my family will be perfect.
Truth: There is no such thing as a perfect family.

"supposed" to do. As far as I can tell, there are no perfect families in the scriptures! On the contrary, the scriptures are filled with families who struggled and were even quite dysfunctional! The children of Lehi and Sariah literally tried to kill each other. My kids only jokingly *threaten* to do that!

If our families are already supposed to be perfect (which is not the case in this life), we wouldn't be learning and growing. *We are families in training.* The scriptures teach us that learning and growing are two of the great opportunities in this life. If family life was without struggle, we wouldn't learn how to love. It's easy to love children who are angelic and who do everything you want them to and who make you look good. But you *really* learn how to love when you have kids who are screaming that they hate you or doing things you don't agree with or like.

Pull out your scriptures if you feel you're not good enough as a parent. The scriptures are very comforting. *Goodly* parents is what we're going for—and by that I mean "good enough." Good-enough parents care about their children. If you pray for your children and try your best to teach them the right way and show them love, you are a *goodly* parent. You can and will expand your parenting toolbox and continue to learn by trial and error. You will have struggles that will teach you valuable life lessons. But right now you can be *goodly,* and you've got to let that be good enough for now.

Learning More about Emotional Family History

I've created a simple outline for doing your emotional family history using the acronym F-A-M-I-L-Y.

F = Get **F**eedback from outsiders

A = **A**sk hard questions

M = Learn your **M**ental health history

I = **I**dentify emotional rules
L = Discover **L**earned life scripts
Y = Examine **Y**our experiences

F—Get Feedback from Outsiders

An *outsider* is anyone who did not grow up in your family but who is exposed to your family dynamics. This can include spouses, in-laws, friends, and neighbors. Due to the obvious fact that you grew up with your family, it's easy to think that the way you saw the day-to-day managing of emotions was the normal way. I'm not saying your experience wasn't normal—but just as a fish is not aware of the water in which it swims, you are often not aware of the emotional environment in which you grew up because it was the only environment you ever knew. Observations from trusted outsiders might help you understand your family patterns a little bit better.

Some examples of observations from outsiders might be things like "It seems your dad has to trump everything you say" or "You get along so well with your siblings." The observations of others can sometimes help you more objectively pinpoint the cause of your struggles because outsiders can see your family patterns with fresh eyes. Whether the feedback is positive or negative, it's worth considering. Maybe what is normal to you really isn't normal, and others can point that out.

Pause and Reflect: Feedback from Outsiders

Think of a situation where someone gave you feedback or made an observation about you or your family that was difficult to hear. Describe the situation here.

_____

_____

_____

_____

What truth or insight is there to what they that person was saying, and how can it be of benefit to you?

_____

_____

_____

_____

What positive quality has someone pointed out about your family that you have perhaps taken for granted?

_____

_____

_____

_____

A—Ask Hard Questions

Be willing to ask the hard questions about family relationship patterns. For example: "Why did Grandma and Grandpa divorce after thirty-eight years?" "When did Uncle Joe and Aunt Betty stop talking to each other?" "How did Uncle Kevin manage to remain so kind and loving even after he returned from the war?" Notice both positive and difficult trends among family members and see what you can learn from them.

Pause and Reflect—What Can I Learn from the Hard Facts?

What can you learn from members of your family who've exhibited incredible capacity for forgiveness, tolerance of differences, or emotional resilience after traumatic experiences?

_____

_____

_____

_____

What can you learn from family issues of unresolved trauma, addictions, abuse, divorces, infidelity, suicide, or other problems that many families don't openly talk about?

_____

_____

_____

_____

M—Learn Your Mental Health History

Just as health histories are important sources of information, the mental health histories of your family can also empower you to be educated, to know what symptoms to watch for, and to get help if those symptoms arise in your own life and in the lives of your children. Mental health histories allow you to be proactive and take preventive measures.

Here's an example of how mental health history is important. A client once told me that she was struggling with postpartum depression. Then she said, "Oh, you know, I talked

> **Myth: If we don't talk about things, they aren't real.**
> **Truth: Problems are real, but if we don't talk about them we don't know what we are dealing with or how to get help.**

with my mom and she said she struggled with postpartum depression too." That would have been a nice conversation to have had with her mother *before* she had a baby. If her mom had said, "I struggled with depression after delivery. You might want to watch for these signs," her daughter would probably have identified and addressed her depression earlier.

Pause and Reflect: Mental Health History

Identify any history of depression, anxiety, personality disorders, substance abuse, physical abuse, sexual abuse, or other struggles in your family.

_____

_____

_____

_____

What did you learn by talking with family members about their struggles that might help you understand yourself better?

_____

_____

_____

_____

I—Identify Emotional Rules

Each family has a unique way of relating, of managing emotions, and of getting emotional needs met. While some of these rules are explicitly talked about ("Men are always right," "We don't talk about feelings," "We wear our feelings on our sleeve," "Never admit that you're wrong," "It's only okay to cry when you're physically hurt"), other rules are only implied, and we follow those rules without conscious awareness. If you were raised with parents who were sensitive to your emotions and needs, then you will likely have healthier emotional rules by which to live.

Pause and Reflect: Emotional Rules

What messages did you receive about expressing and feeling happiness, sadness, anger, fright, surprise, disgust/shame?

_____

_____

_____

_____

How did your parents manage intense emotions of their own?
Mom:

_____

_____

_____

_____

Dad:

_____

_____

_____

_____

How did your family respond when you expressed each of these emotions?
Happiness:

_____

_____

_____

Anger:

_____

_____

_____

Sadness:

_____

_____

_____

Fright:

_____

_____

_____

Surprise/Excitement:

_____

_____

_____

Disgust/Shame:

_____

_____

_____

L—Discover Learned Life Scripts

Similar to a movie script, you learn who your "character" is "supposed" to be in your family. For example, you may play the part of the smart one, or the pretty one, or the black sheep, or a combination of characters.

You also learn what the acceptable and unacceptable responses are in certain situations. For example, when someone says you did a great job on a project at work, your learned life script says you are supposed to point out all of the flaws in your presentation and discount the compliment so as not to appear haughty or make others feel inferior.

You also live by scripts regarding your physical body, money, intelligence, worth, future, gender role, intimate relationships, sexuality, and family life. Just like emotional rules, many of the scripts you live by are implied through the actions of those in your home. These rules may never have been stated directly. For example, if your parents never discussed sex with you, you may be living by a script that tells you sex is bad and wrong and not something to be talked about.

It's important to recognize which characters and scripts you are caught up in, however complex they might be. Some roles may have been written for you before you ever arrived. While it may seem to be the way it's always been, it doesn't have to continue that way. Once you become aware of those patterns, you can make different choices.

Pause and Reflect: Learned Life Scripts

What "character" do you play in your family story?

_____

_____

_____

_____

Think of a life script that you learned in your family of origin that you want to keep.

_____

_____

_____

_____

Think of a life script that you learned in your family of origin that you want to change in your own life.

_____

_____

_____

_____

Y—Examine Your Experiences

The beauty of becoming aware of your emotional history is that you are now free to sift through the information, keep the positive emotional patterns, and be proactive in changing the patterns you don't want to pass on to your family. Knowledge allows you to take action in your current and future emotional life. For example, if your family has anger management issues and you find yourself losing your temper with your family, take anger management classes or consult a therapist.

Again, the purpose of doing your emotional history is *not* to blame your parents or grandparents for your choices. The purpose is to understand where you came from, what your strengths and obstacles are, and to take charge of your own life.

Pause and Reflect: Valuing Your Experiences

Examine, reflect, and write about your own experiences in your family—the positive and the painful. Take the emotional family history information you receive from others and check it against your own experience in your family. Ask yourself, "Does this fit with my experiences?"

CURE 4: TAKE RESPONSIBILITY FOR YOUR OWN HAPPINESS

WOMEN IN MY THERAPY OFFICE frequently complain, "I'm working so hard and doing so many good things and trying so hard to be a faithful woman. Why am I unhappy?" That's a good question. It has jokingly been said that if "men are, that they might have joy" (2 Ne. 2:25), then women are that they might have guilt!

I'm totally kidding.

Women also are that they might have joy, and yet some of us have decided along the way that it's more "righteous" to feel like a martyr. In this chapter we will explore some cultural beliefs that rob us of the joy that is the design of our existence: "If I take good care of myself I'm being selfish," "Other people or circumstances will *make* me happy," and "I don't have time to do the things that bring me joy."

President Dieter F. Uchtdorf urges all of us who are busy, weary, or discouraged to remember that happiness is our birthright and that the purpose of our great voyage to this earth. Wisely, President Uchtdorf counsels that in our hectic world it is very normal to feel overwhelmed by emotions of suffering and sorrow. He points out that there is not a simple switch we can flip to stop negative feelings of distress and acknowledges that our trials are very real and can be extremely difficult. But he admonishes us to remember that God loves us and will help us—and that part of our divine heritage is happiness for this earth-life and for the eternities (see Dieter F. Uchtdorf, "Happiness, Your Heritage," *Ensign*, October 2008). This thought of having a heritage of happiness helps me to have the hope I need to simply survive some days.

Whenever I introduce the divine concept of taking responsibility for our own happiness in my workshops, I like to hold up a pair of running shoes as a visual aid. I ask the audience how they think a pair of running shoes relates to preventing emotional burnout. Once a participant yelled out, "Run away!" While it's true that we may find ourselves wanting to lace up our shoes and run away from our lives, the shoe actually stands for taking responsibility for your own happiness. You're the only one walking in your shoes, after all. Nobody can walk your path for you, stand in your place, or take the

Myth: Taking good care of myself is selfish.
Truth: Taking care of myself is *smart* and *necessary* for a *selfless* life.

steps that you need to take to become the kind of divine, joy-full person God knows you to be.

About ten years ago I received a letter from a young mom named Kim, who had attended one of my workshops earlier that year. As a new mother with two girls—a newborn and an eighteen-month-old—she was in survival mode, feeling physically weak, spiritually lost, and emotionally depleted. She said, "I was taking care of my kids and husband but I wasn't really taking care of myself."

During that particular workshop I shared that I'd recently accomplished a personal goal of running a marathon. As I talked about my experience, Kim felt impressed to listen. Feeling inspired to take better care of herself, she decided that she too wanted to train for a marathon, and she felt that this goal was about much more than physical fitness. Kim said, "When I started out, I had no idea what an amazing process it would be for me." She completed her first marathon and sent me a card. She also wrote about what she had gained from taking responsibility for her happiness:

I feel more confident in my body. I'm healthier. My marriage improved as my husband supported me in my training. When I come back after running, I'm more excited to be with my girls, and I'm more patient with them because I'm taking better care of me. Spiritually, I've rediscovered my testimony along the way. I remember running in silence and feeling the Spirit, watching the sunrise. I'm closer to God because I pray while running alone. I invited my sisters to run with me, and through our training we became best friends, sharing our hearts, the ups and downs of family life, sometimes running with tears streaming down our faces.

In addition to taking better care of herself, Kim learned that she could do hard things, even through obstacles like a knee injury! This self-confidence has helped her to continue to prioritize taking good care of herself. She *did* something about the fact that she was feeling blah about her life. She didn't wait for her children to grow up to make her feel better. She didn't wait for her husband to rescue her from her emptiness and dissatisfaction with life.

Kim's experience illustrates how taking responsibility for your own happiness is actually a gift to yourself and your loved ones and can bring you closer to Heavenly Father.

I realize that not everyone wants to, is able to, or will ever run a marathon. For most of us, just living life is marathon enough. The point is not to pick up competitive running as a physical pursuit, but to realize that there are important things each of us can do for ourselves. If the running shoes don't work for you, adapt the concept to something that does work in your life: hiking shoes, swimming goggles, a yoga pose, even the Book of Mormon if reading it more will help you be healthier and bring greater joy.

Selfish versus Selfless

When I talk about the importance of taking care of yourself, I'm often met with the concern about being selfish. Who wants to be selfish? After all, we are followers of Jesus Christ, the most selfless person who walked the earth. We are trying to be like Him and serve others.

The root of the word *selfless* is *self.* In order to have "less of a self" you have to first have a self. In other words, you have to have a self before you can offer it—you can't give up something you don't have. I sometimes demonstrate this in my workshop by getting help from someone in the front row. I hold up a small ball and say, "Joanne, please give me this ball."

Confused and a little embarrassed, she says, "I can't."

I ask teasingly, "Why not?"

She says, "Because I don't have it. I'm not holding it."

I say with a sneaky grin, "Exactly."

Then we start all over. I throw her the ball and ask, "Joanne, will you give me the ball?" She throws it back to me.

Silly example, but it's an important point: Joanne can't offer something she doesn't have, and neither can you or I! We can feel emotionally burned out when trying to be selfless without first having invested in a joyful *self* to offer. We just give and give because we are supposed to, but if we don't know who we are or what our strengths and limitations are, we may end up feeling lost and empty.

Your "self" is all of the things that make you *you*. Most central to your sense of self is your unique and eternal spirit. Your "self" also includes your thoughts, feelings, gifts, dreams, desires, and experiences. Becoming your best and most authentic self requires taking time to invest energy into your own personal development, which is part of the process of becoming selfless.

Prophets have frequently encouraged personal development of education and talents. For example, Gordon B. Hinckley said to the young women of the Church, "I must remind you that you must get all of the education that you possibly can. Life has become so complex and competitive. You cannot assume that you have entitlements due you. You will be expected to put forth great effort and to use your best talents to make your way to the most wonderful future of which you are capable" (Gordon B. Hinckley, "Stay on the High Road," *Ensign*, May 2004, 113).

Signs of a Healthy Self

You might be asking, "What is a healthy self?" and "How do I know if I have developed it?"

From my experience as a psychotherapist, there are several hallmarks of people who haven't invested in developing a strong sense of who they are—and, by comparison, I can also identify traits and characteristics that indicate a person does have a well-developed sense of self.

Most of us are in a process of developing ourselves in different facets of life. There might be areas of your life where you are completely confident and other areas where you feel weak and small. But just to give you a general idea of the differences, I've created a list that compares traits that fall at each end of the spectrum; obviously, there are aspects that overlap in the middle somewhere.

Weak Sense of Self
- Others have too much say in directing your life; you feel as if "my life lives me."
- You are on an emotional roller coaster; your emotions are dictated by or greatly affected by others' opinions, emotions, and input. You take on the feelings of others around you; their feelings become yours (for example, "My roommate had a bad day, so my day is also bad").
- You lack a clear sense of priorities and preferences. You tend to go along with whatever others want; you lack your own opinions—"I don't care what we do tonight. I'll do whatever you want."
- You have difficulty making decisions for fear of doing something wrong or letting others down; you feel paralyzed and unable to take action in life. The bigger the decision, the less able you are to make a choice.
- You might have the following recurring thoughts: "I don't know what I want," "I'm not sure how I feel," "I don't know what I want and even if I did, it doesn't matter."
- You fear being alone. Being all by yourself is really uncomfortable to you.

- You like being alone because you want to avoid others due to weak or fragile sense of self.
- You're a chameleon—you're into whatever someone else is into, you try to be like or imitate others, or you easily change your own opinion in the presence of someone stronger.

Strong Sense of Self
- You consider the opinions of others, but ultimately you know you have the final say in your life.
- You have an awareness of how you feel and are able to empathize with the feelings of others, but you don't take on the feelings of others as your own.
- You allow others to feel how they feel. You can comfort and help them through a hard time without being overwhelmed by their emotional state (for example, when your roommate has a bad day, you give her a hug, listen to her, and invite her out to dinner with some mutual friends).
- You have a clear sense of your priorities and preferences. You tend to do what is important to you but are also able to negotiate or compromise if needed. You can express your own opinions and input but respect that other people have their input and opinions too.
- You can make difficult decisions and you accept responsibility for the outcome. You are able to take risks in life with a realistic view.
- You might have the following recurring thoughts: "This is what I think . . ." "I know how I feel," "I know what I want and it's my job to make it happen."
- You enjoy your own company and the company of others.
- You're adaptable but you know there are certain things you won't compromise because of their importance to you. Your opinions and values are consistent no matter who you are talking to.

Strengthening Your Self

If you rate yourself closer to the weak sense of self description, there are several things you can do to strengthen your sense of self. These suggestions can help you stretch, grow, and discover more about who you are and what is important to you. Many of these ideas will foster opportunities to go outside of your comfort zone or challenge limiting views about who you are and what you are capable of doing.

If you tend to avoid being alone, schedule regular alone time. For example, take yourself out to dinner or to a movie. If your tendency is to avoid other people, build in regular social opportunities, such as taking a class or getting involved in a club or group. Notice the feelings and thoughts that come up as you venture out of your comfort zone and use that information as a catalyst for your own inner growth.

Ask yourself the questions you would ask another person you have just met and want to learn more about. How do you spend your free time? What kind of food do you like? What kinds of recreational activities appeal to you? What is your favorite book? What kind of music do you listen to? What's the saddest thing that's ever happened to you? What is the most joyful experience you've had? What are your dreams?

Do things that challenge your assumptions about yourself. For example, if you think you're not a good swimmer, take a swimming class. If you're scared of starting a business, start researching what it would take. If nobody in your family has gone to college, consider signing up for a college course. If you can't go out of the house without makeup, do it once as an act of courage and strength. If you've worn the same hairstyle your whole life, go get a new cut. You get the idea.

Change up your normal routine and expand your awareness of the world around you. There are certain opportunities that are great catalysts for inner growth, such as going on a mission, going away to college, taking the next step in your education, going to another country, or teaching and serving different populations or underprivileged communities. Take advantage of those opportunities as they present themselves.

Tune in to your emotional life and get curious about learning more about what makes you tick. Notice and be aware of your emotions, note what you gravitate toward or avoid, and pay attention to your body's cues.

Redefining Selfish

In my quest to unravel this tricky relationship between self-selfish-selfless, I looked up the word *selfish* in the dictionary and had one of those light-bulb moments of clarity. According to Merriam-Webster, *selfish* means "Seeking or concentrating on one's own advantage, pleasure, or well-being without regard for others." Selfishness is doing what's in your own best interest *without* regard for others. So is doing what's in your best interest *with* regard for others selfish? Or does that describe self-care? I am of the opinion that doing what's in your best interest *with regard for others* is simply taking good care of yourself. That means developing who you are, what you believe, what your talents are, and being a steward of the gifts that Heavenly Father has given you so you have more to offer others. It's important to know who you are! But many women disregard their own interests because they mistakenly believe that doing *anything* for themselves is selfish.

Here are additional examples to clarify self-care with regard for others as opposed to selfish disregard for others.

<u>Buying a new outfit</u>
Self-care: Saving up to buy the outfit.
Selfish: Buying a dress on a whim with grocery money.

<u>Exercising</u>
Self-care: Prioritizing exercise and planning with your spouse to exercise when he can be home with the children.
Selfish: Leaving young children unattended at home so you can go on a run.

<u>Expressing anger and sadness about feeling under-appreciated by your family</u>
Self-care: Responsibly sharing your feelings with your family and asking your family at dinner, in FHE, or in person for more validation and appreciation.
Selfish: Making sarcastic comments during dinner about how ungrateful your family is and how you *always* do *everything*.

<u>Taking a nap</u>
Self-care: Setting your alarm so you don't miss your visiting teaching appointment.
Selfish: Sleeping through your visiting teaching appointment.

<u>Taking an art class</u>
Self-care: Taking an intensive summer art class through a local university.
Selfish: Taking a month sabbatical to Italy to study with a world-renowned artist without notifying your boss that you'll be gone for a month.

Things That Only You Can Do

Wouldn't it be great if we could borrow self-care from others? "I have too much to do. Will you sleep a few extra hours for me tonight, honey?"

Survey: Exercise versus Exhaustion

50 percent of women surveyed reported that they feel tired or worried most of the time.

48 percent of women surveyed reported that they exercise three times a week for half an hour.

47 percent of women surveyed reported that they get less than seven hours of sleep per night.

"I ate too many cookies. Best friend, will you put your five-mile run in *my* exercise account?"

The large group of women I surveyed is just slightly below the average when compared to the number of Americans who exercise regularly. In 2010, 51.1 percent of Americans reported exercising for least thirty minutes three or more days per week (see Elizabeth Mendes at Gallup.com, February 16, 2001). And when it comes to sleep, many LDS women tend not to follow the Centers for Disease Control recommendation of seven to nine hours of sleep per night (see Centers for Disease Control, *Sleep and Sleep Disorders*, CDC.gov).

There are certain things to prevent burnout that only you can do for yourself. Others can support you in your efforts but it's ultimately it's up to you. Here's a partial list:

Physical—eat well, exercise, manage your stress, take care of your body, work on your goals

Spiritual—pray; study scriptures; develop a personal relationship with God the Father, His Son Jesus Christ, and the Holy Ghost; hear spiritual promptings; forgive; develop your testimony

Emotional—feel your feelings, make sense of your feelings, manage your emotions, let go of resentment, reflect on experiences, feel satisfied in life

Relational—be a friend to someone, be a wife to your spouse, be a mother to your children, resolve your relationship distresses, apologize for your mistakes or missteps, express your love

Intellectual—study things out in your mind, learn your life lessons, think your thoughts, learn, increase your knowledge, get your education

---

Survey: Time Management

51 percent of women surveyed report they don't have enough time to pursue their own interests and meet their own needs.

No matter how busy you are, there are still things that no one else can do for you, nor can anyone else but you decide to pursue what's important to you.

If you're not meeting your own needs, who is going to? Your children? Your neighbor? Your best friend? Your siblings? Maybe your husband? Your Church leader? Whose job is it to meet *your* needs?

If *you* are not seeing to it that your needs are met, your needs are not likely going to be met. Your interests and talents won't be developed because nobody else can do that for you. I've noticed that when we are not taking care of ourselves, we look to other people to fill us up. And when others don't meet our emotional needs or fill our emotional bucket, we get resentful.

Dependence Breeds Hostility

One of my college professors said, "Dependence breeds hostility." Many people believe that they can't be happy unless they get a certain outcome in life or relationships by having, for example, financial security, a husband, obedient children, someone's forgiveness or approval, a bigger house, a more prestigious calling, a raise, or any other external outcome that we

Myth: The people who love me will make sure I'm happy. Truth: No one can *make* you happy. That's your job.

think we need in order to be happy or feel good. I've observed that as long as we *expect* those things to make us happy, we become resentful if we *don't* get those things. Why? Because nobody or no thing outside of us has the power to make us happy, though they can add to our existing happiness or provide temporary enjoyment. If you are unhappy, you'll probably be unhappy no matter what happens to you or for you. The opposite is also usually true. People who are truly happy can't usually be stripped of their peace by negative circumstances or events. For example, Victor Frankl, Mother Teresa, and Ghandi all lived in unfavorable and even painful conditions but still found a way to be joyful.

I have seen this pattern in my therapy practice, particularly with women who look to their family relationships to make them happy. Years ago I counseled a talented young adult we'll call Sarah. Sarah's mother had made it very clear to Sarah that if she didn't meet her mother's expectations—whether excelling in piano, dating the right boys, or wearing certain clothes—her mother would feel that she had personally done something wrong and was a failure as a mother—her most important calling. Sarah felt so responsible for her mother's self-esteem that she was racked with guilt for wanting to do things her own way. Her mom had looked to Sarah to give her feelings of self-esteem and to prove that she was a good mother. Sarah became rigidly obedient, fearful of making any mistakes, and scared to express any emotions that might upset her mother. By not taking responsibility for her own happiness, the mother was looking to Sarah for her self-esteem. Sarah and her mother had both become resentful of each other because neither was getting what she wanted because her personal happiness ultimately depended or hinged on another person and was not grounded in herself.

While you may want the help and support of loved ones in order to take good care of yourself, you can't put the responsibility for *providing* happiness, joy, or fulfillment on anybody else. No one else can make you happy. That's your job. The key lesson to remember here is that people can change and you can learn to find ways to be happy even in difficult times; each of us can learn to endure life *well*.

Follow Your Bliss

A crucial way to prevent emotional burnout is by investing in your own happiness and joy and pursuing the things that excite you about your life. Well-known American writer and mythologist Joseph Campbell said that if you "follow your bliss, you put yourself on a kind of track that has been there all the while, waiting for you, and the life that you ought to be living is the one you are living . . . Follow your bliss and don't be afraid, and doors will open where you didn't know they were going to be" (Joseph Campbell, *The Power of Myth* [New York: Anchor Books, 1988], 150).

I believe that feelings of happiness, joy, and bliss are ways that a loving God can nudge us in a certain direction, providing crucial information about our life missions. I say *missions* (plural) after years of working with therapy clients who are fearful that they've missed their one and only life mission due to mistakes or detours they've taken. I find it comforting to think that our loving Heavenly Father may have many possible missions for us, and we need

> ### Workshop Comments:
> ### What Brought Joy as a Child?
>
> - Playing softball
> - New shoes
> - Reading
> - Riding a bicycle
> - Being in the mountains
> - Hamburgers
> - Vacations
> - Running through sprinklers
> - Swimming with cousins
> - Listening to my mom play the piano
> - Crafts
> - Music
> - Grandma's house
> - Dancing
> - Horseback riding
> - Walking on the beach
> - Blowing bubbles
> - Jumping in the leaves
> - Painting
> - Running and playing games outside
> - Being tossed into the air by someone I loved and trusted, knowing they would catch me
> - Making forts outside and preparing feasts of bark, petals, leaves, and acorns

not fear that we've missed out on our one chance to make a difference in the world. No matter what we do in life, the Lord can strengthen us and turn our stumbling blocks into stepping-stones of growth. He has the power to help us and will provide the way for us to accomplish what He has in store. Remember, we *are* that we might have *joy*! (See 2 Ne. 2:25.)

Sometimes we have childlike joy about a particular activity but as we get older the joys and passions we once had get suppressed or subdued. Some of us may abandon them entirely. But you can't ignore the fact that there were things that once brought great joy. Maybe the thing that brought you joy seems impractical to pursue as an adult, but I invite you to open up, explore, and recover what that is for you. You never know where it will lead you.

Ever since I was a little girl I've loved to sing—not just for the attention or applause, but because it has always brought me joy. One of my favorite childhood experiences was standing on the piano bench with the lights dimmed and singing at the top of my lungs while my dad (professional composer and musician Lex de Azevedo) spontaneously played my song requests. I had my very own human Karaoke machine! That was pure joy.

At one point in my young-adult life, something changed. Music became an obligation. I had transitioned into writing, performing, and recording professionally, which changed how I felt about music for a while. Instead of joy, I felt stress and pressure to meet others' expectations. I had shifted my own expectations of myself, which left me rarely feeling good enough, talented enough, thin enough, polished enough, skilled enough. Weighty expectations had clouded the bliss that I used to feel when singing and playing piano. I struggled with the fear that I wouldn't measure up. I decided to take a break from music as a profession so I could rediscover the bliss I once had. Music used to be a way to be fully engaged in the moment, lost in the creative process. I had to remember how to write and sing for *me,* for my own joy, instead of for an audience. When I finally resumed music professionally, I was able to maintain the joy I'd rediscovered. Staying connected with that joy allows me to offer so much more of myself to others as a songwriter and performer.

So let's explore *your* childhood bliss. What brought you joy as a child?

Pause and Reflect: What Brought You Joy as a Child?

List five things that brought you joy as a child. They can be simple and small.

1. _____

2. _____

3. _____

4. _____

5. _____

Reclaiming Childhood Joy

Look at the list you just made. I want to challenge you to bring at least one thing on that list back into your life in some way, even if it requires you to get a bit creative. Maybe you wrote *climbing trees*, but you have bad knees. While you may not be able to climb trees, you can still take your neighbors' kids or your nieces or grandkids go to the park and watch them climb. If you don't have children or grandchildren of your own, chances are there are several children in your ward or neighborhood who would love an outing to the park or a friendly backyard (and parents who might enjoy a bit of a break!). Volunteer through your school district at a local school—most would be very happy to have a helping hand. The point is, bring it back somehow. You'll be amazed at the joy that comes from reconnecting with something you loved as a child.

Think about the words *recreation* (*leisurely* activities) and *re-creation* (creating something all over again). Taking time to do something that you love and that brings joy re-creates your spirit, generates vitality, and re-energizes your emotional life. And remember, you are the only person who can re-create that inner experience of joy.

Another one of my "blisses" is being in the sun and water. I grew up in Southern California, where we had a pool and my grandma had a pool—it seemed like everyone had one. That feeling of summer in the pool just brings me joy. I always have to make that happen. Since I now live in Utah, the summers here are nice and hot, but I usually have to get out of town in the winter and escape to somewhere sunny so I can lie by the pool in the sun. It makes me so happy.

One workshop participant told me about bringing her joy of dancing back into her life:

I love to dance but as a working mother I've had to get creative. It's not realistic for me to spend hours at a dance studio like I did when I was single, so last year Santa brought me "Just Dance" on the Wii. As a mom it brings me joy because I am dancing, and also because my children get to see me in a different light.

The things that bring happiness are important because they teach us about why we're on the planet. Very early on, I loved connecting and learning about people and expressing myself through music. When asked by my kindergarten teacher to paint what I wanted to be when I grew up, I painted a mom holding a baby in one arm and a small child in the other with the words

"When I grow up I want to be a mommy." I still have that picture to this day; it's framed on my wall. The things that made my heart sing as a little girl foreshadowed some aspects of my life's missions.

I challenge you to integrate your early joys into your adult life somehow and see what happens! You will feel more alive and you will have more abundance to share with others. For example, many of us probably enjoyed sending and receiving letters and gifts in the mail. If you haven't written a meaningful letter lately, try sending a few of them out. My guess is you'll likely receive one or two back. If you enjoy correspondence with your children, especially if they are teenagers or young adults, chances are you'll have to take a leap in technology; try using e-mail, texting, or one of the many social media sites on the Internet. I know plenty of women in their seventies who have learned how to use these technologies and have found that they are easy and delightful ways to correspond with loved ones.

> **Workshop Comments: Your Life List**
>
> Once you've remembered the things that brought you joy, think about one thing you want to do before you die—something on your bucket list, or your life list. Here are some things that the women in my workshops wanted to do before they "kicked the bucket":
>
> - Go to Hawaii
> - Write a book
> - Sky dive
> - Go on a mission with my husband
> - Visit all fifty states
> - Stay healthy
> - Paint a picture
> - Go to Nauvoo
> - Bike tour through Ireland
> - Spend a week in New York
> - Get married
> - Run a race
> - Learn how to sew
> - Get a master's degree
> - Sing a solo

Pause and Reflect: What Can Bring You Joy Now?

List five ways you can incorporate the things that brought you joy as a child into your current life. You may have to get a bit creative!

1. _____

2. _____

3. _____

4. _____

5. _____

What do your answers teach you about your life's missions?

_____

_____

_____

_____

_____

_____

I think it's important to have something to look forward to as a way of maintaining a sense of joy in your life. Whatever your future dreams, wishes, or desires are, think about one thing you can do now, one step toward one of those goals. Take one step. If your goal is to write a book, come up with an outline, jot down some things about the plot, or start journaling. If your dream is to go to Nauvoo, put all your change into a piggy bank. There are things you can be doing for your goals right now, and I challenge you to actually take a step toward one of those goals. It may not happen for a long time but it won't happen at all if you are not heading toward it.

Pause and Reflect: Create a Life List

List five goals you want to accomplish or five dreams you want to fulfill in your life.

1. _____

2. _____

3. _____

4. _____

5. _____

What is one step you can take to fulfill each dream?

1. _____

2. _____

3. _____

4. _____
5. _____

In addition to engaging in activities that bring you joy, your emotional health depends on learning how to actively engage in feeling joy on a regular basis, no matter what your current situation.

Take Responsibility for Your View

While you might be comfortable with the idea that you have to do things to take care of yourself, it may be harder to overcome the trials in your life that others have inflicted upon you, intentionally or not. Although we teach and value forgiveness, many struggle to know exactly how to let go of anger, resentment, pain, and suffering—especially if the effects of someone's actions are long-lasting. I'd like to offer some helpful perspectives and tools that will help you forgive those who have wronged you.

A helpful definition of forgiveness is "ceasing to feel resentment." There is an old Buddhist saying: "Holding onto anger is like drinking poison and expecting the other person to die." Forgiving others who have wronged you deeply can be extremely difficult; however, you can do it with the Lord's help. And if you do, it will be as though you are cleansed or purified of something toxic, a caustic part of your life that continually cankers your soul. But before you can rid yourself of that anger and resentment, you have to recognize it as such and deal with it through genuine forgiveness that can make you heal— make you whole. Similar to the example of how you have to have a self before you can give it up, it's important to *feel* your feelings before you can let them go.

Forgiveness Doesn't Mean that What Happened Was Okay

Holding onto resentment and hurt contributes to emotional burnout and robs you of the joy that can be yours in this life. While we all believe in the concept of forgiveness, actually *doing* it is a skill and an art that needs to be practiced. I've worked with many clients who've had difficulty forgiving someone because they believe that forgiving someone means they approve of the other person's action. Forgiveness isn't about condoning someone else's behavior. Nor does forgiveness mean that you have to completely forget about another person's behavior, especially if it is potentially harmful. Forgiveness is about *you* refusing to let past pain rule *your* future. It's accepting that bad stuff happens to everyone and that you can heal and move forward with your life.

You can forgive an abuser and still press charges.

You can forgive your spouse for being unfaithful but you don't have to stay married.

You can forgive a child who is addicted to drugs and stealing from you but you don't have to let that child live in your home.

Things Are Not Always What They Seem

In my own life and through my clients' struggles, I've noticed something quite interesting. People often carry hurt and pain *not* from the actual events that were hurtful, but because of the conclusions they draw about the events. In other words, something painful might have happened to you in the past; you keep the pain alive by adopting stressful viewpoints about yourself and your life and live them as a self-fulfilling prophecy.

For example, imagine a coworker who was jealous of your accomplishments went to your boss and made false accusations about your character. This caused problems for you: you had to endure an uncomfortable meeting with your boss to get the whole mess straightened out, and it created some stress for you to have to talk about this coworker. Let's say your reputation is now restored with your boss, but in anger you decide, "People just can't be trusted." You decide to simply go to work every day and avoid that coworker. Which is more painful—the discomfort caused by that one meeting with your boss, or a lifetime of believing that people can't be trusted? The latter will do much more damage to your relationships because if you firmly believe that people can't be trusted, you may be perpetually skeptical, defensive, and guarded.

Sometimes it's hard to separate the facts from the interpretation, so let me clarify further with the same example.

Facts
- Coworker said things to my boss about me
- Boss talked to me
- Sat in a meeting with my boss
- Boss talked and I listened
- I talked and boss listened
- I felt feelings of discomfort
- My heart started beating faster, my palms became sweaty
- I got a headache
- Meeting ended

Possible Interpretations
- My coworker is out to get me
- My coworker makes me so angry sometimes
- I'm going to get in trouble
- My boss doesn't trust me

- I have to be careful around here
- My job is on the line
- If I lose my job, then I'll be a failure
- I have to prove my worth
- My coworker is jealous of me and is trying to get me in trouble
- The facts are pretty boring; the stress and drama reside in the conclusions.

Better Interpretations

But . . . it's also possible to conclude, from the same situation:
- My boss is really committed to me and my career because he cares enough to address this.
- I am a valued employee and I'm glad he gave me a chance to clear things up.
- My coworker must be experiencing a lot of fear and insecurity right now; I wonder how I can help her.

You cannot change what happened because it's in the past. However, you can get out of pain faster if you *accept responsibility* for the fact that your mind and heart added interpretations that compounded your painful situation. If you can practice mentally separating the facts from your interpretation of the facts, you'll discover that it's not only possible to add the meaning you want to anything that happens, you'll also find that most of us develop habits of interpreting certain kinds of interactions, events, and circumstances. If that's the case, why not add meaning that opens up your heart and mind instead of weighing you down?

Your interpretation of your life is simply *your* view and not necessarily the whole picture. While your perspective may be valid and easily justified, you have to realize that there are hundreds of other viewpoints that you could adopt if you open your mind to seeing your circumstances in a different light. Another way of saying this is that while there are objective facts and absolutes in life and certainly in our doctrinal beliefs, there is also some real validity in our own individual subjectivity—in your own personal way of acting and reacting as you choose how to live your life.

Here is a little tool for helping that process along.

Pause and Reflect: Facts and Interpretation

Think of a situation you are currently or were recently upset about.

_____

_____

_____

_____

What are the facts?

_____

_____

_____

_____

What interpretations did you ascribe to the situation?

_____

_____

_____

What are two *other* possible and plausible conclusions you could draw from the same facts?

_____

_____

_____

_____

Consider taking greater responsibility for how you view or interpret events that happen to you. It's amazing how freeing it is to realize that even if you have been deeply hurt, you can choose another interpretation by which to live more freely. Feel and then let go of emotions that weigh you down or drain your emotional energy.

CURE 5: PRACTICE BEING KIND TO YOURSELF

The fifth suggestion for preventing emotional burnout is to practice being kind to yourself. In my experience, women often treat others in a much kinder manner than they treat themselves. It can be something as simple as taking bubble bath at night to wind down or feeling empathy toward yourself after making a mistake.

Self-compassion researcher Dr. Kristin Neff defines self-kindness as being "gentle and understanding with ourselves rather than harshly critical and judgmental." Self-kindness is one of three aspects of developing and practicing self-compassion.

Practicing Self-Compassion: Kinder Thoughts, Better Feelings

Practicing self-compassion requires us to *recognize* our own suffering and then to *respond* to ourselves in thoughts and actions as kindly as you would respond to a loved one. The second aspect of self-compassion, according to Neff, is cultivating a feeling of common humanity, or the sense that our imperfections and pain are what connects us to others. Mindfulness, the final aspect of developing self-compassion, is simply seeing and accepting "what is" without criticism or judgment (see Kristin Neff, *Self-compassion: Stop Beating Yourself Up and Leave Insecurity Behind* [New York: HarperCollins, 2011], 41).

Being compassionate and kind to themselves is a struggle for many women. Many of us have heard that we should try to give children two or three compliments for every criticism—even constructive criticism. People need more positive feedback and input to outweigh the heavy weight of negativity in their lives. New research is showing that we need a three-to-one ratio of positive to negative and that resilient, happy people not only feel a feel a broad range of emotion, they also find ways to experience as many positive emotions as possible (see Elaine Fox, *Rainy Brain Sunny Brain* [New York: Basic Books, 2012], 197).

If you pay attention to your self-talk—the thoughts you have about yourself—you might realize that somewhere between 60 and 85 percent of what you say to yourself is negative. If you said the same negative things out loud to others that you say to yourself, no one would want to be around you! And yet many of us say unkind, critical, harsh, and judgmental things to ourselves every day.

Here's an example to help you become more aware of what you say to yourself. During a conversation with somebody that you really respect and admire—say your boss or your church leader—imagine that you say something so embarrassing that you wish you could just crawl in a hole.

For example, you ask, "Oh, are you expecting?"

The other person responds, "No, my baby is two years old."

You might walk away from that situation saying something to yourself such as:

How could I be so stupid!
I'm so dumb!
I can't believe I did it again!
Open mouth. Insert foot.
I will never open my mouth again.
That was stupid!

Workshop Comments: What Do I Think of My Physical Self?

Imagine standing in front of a full-length mirror and taking a long, hard look at yourself. Imagine standing there for five minutes looking at your hair, your face, your skin, your shape, your thighs, your body—front and back. What would you say to yourself? This is how some of my workshop participants responded to this question:

- Scary!
- Eww.
- What happened?
- Fat is in.
- How did that get there?
- Well, there's some proof that gravity is real.
- I need to lose some weight!
- Look at that gross stomach. Yuck!
- Mother, is that you?
- My nose is huge.
- Look at those bags under my eyes!

Would you say any of those things to other people about *their* bodies? I hope not.

Pause and Reflect: Saying Something Embarrassing

Write down a situation where you said something you've regretted.

_____

_____

_____

_____

What did you say to yourself about the situation?

_____

_____

_____

What kinder phrase could you say to yourself instead?

_____

_____

_____

Pause and Reflect: Negative Body Talk

Stand in front of a full-length mirror and look at your body and observe where your thoughts go. Write them here.

_____

_____

_____

_____

What are some kinder messages that you could say to yourself instead?

_____

_____

_____

_____

Now take all that negative self-talk and imagine a three-year-old girl standing in front of you. Picture saying those things to her: "Eww! Disgusting! Gross! I can't believe you said that! You're so stupid! You did it again!" Can you imagine the hurt and pain those things would cause her? So many of us talk to ourselves that way all the time, often without being aware that we do, and then we wonder why we struggle to feel good about ourselves.

I have an image in my mind of that little three-year-old girl buried somewhere inside every grown woman. It's like those little Russian nesting dolls where you open one up and there's another one. She's in there, along with the five-year-old, the eight-year-old, the fifteen-year old, and on up to the fifty-year-old and the eighty-year-old. We all have a vulnerable, sweet child inside. No matter what your age, those kinds of words are hurtful to you. It's so important to practice being kind to *yourself.*

Why is it so easy to be kind to others and notice the good them while it can be so hard to see our own strengths? In his book *Happiness Is a Serious Problem,* Dennis Prager introduces the concept of "The Missing Tile Syndrome" that illustrates our human tendency to focus on what's missing instead of what's present. For example, if you're looking at a ceiling with a tile missing, do you focus on all of the tiles that are there? No. You focus on the missing tile (see Dennis Prager, *Happiness Is a Serious Problem: A Human Nature Repair Manual* [New York: HarperCollins, 1998], 31–32).

We tend to do this with outward characteristics and traits, but I wonder how often we look at the unseen, inner, emotional aspects of our lives and the lives of others. We need to learn to "look" carefully at our inner selves as well as our outer selves. Much like the exercise above with our physical bodies, what if we held mirrors up to our souls? What would catch our attention? What are our emotional, intellectual, and spiritual gifts? What are some aspects of our inner lives that could use improvement?

Pause and Reflect: Strengths and Weaknesses Inside and Out

Quick! In thirty seconds, list ten things you *dislike* about yourself.

1. _____
2. _____
3. _____
4. _____
5. _____
6. _____
7. _____
8. _____
9. _____
10. _____

Now, in thirty seconds, list ten things you *like* about yourself.

1. _____

2. _____

3. _____

4. _____

5. _____

6. _____

7. _____

8. _____

9. _____

10. _____

Which list was easier and quicker to complete? What does that say about your mindset?

_____

_____

_____

_____

What do you think could happen if you give your positive attributes at least equal time in your mind?

_____

_____

_____

_____

If you focus solely on what's missing—on your weaknesses—you will likely not feel as happy as if you focus on your strengths. That doesn't mean that you don't keep working on your weaknesses. You can focus on your personal strengths and good qualities *while* working on the areas of yourself you'd like to improve.

The Guilt Trap

I've been told repeatedly by women who come to my practice that one of the main burdens they carry is guilt. Ironically, most tell me they carry guilty feelings not over things they have done but for things they think they *should* be doing. Many of us have an unhealthy tendency to "could have," "would have," and "should have" ourselves too much.

I wonder if members of our Church are the only ones who feel guilty for the things we *haven't* done! (Of course there are many other religious and cultural traditions that deal with this issue.) At any given moment we can only do one thing, right? (Okay, maybe three things—cooking, nursing the baby, and talking on the phone.) Right now, you are reading this book. That means you are *not* doing your visiting teaching right now, you're not reading stories to your kids right now, you're not organizing your closet right now, and you're not reading your scriptures right now. At any moment there are only a finite number of things you can do, but there is always an *infinite* number of possible things you could or should be doing. That's a bottomless pit that will generate unproductive and chronic feelings of guilt. I believe that our Heavenly Father would rather that we feel good about ourselves *as* we keep improving.

> **Survey: Feeling Guilty**
>
> 81 percent of women surveyed feel guilty for all the things they are *not* doing.

Save Guilt for Sin

While there is always room for improvement in our lives, guilt is not a very good motivator for long-term inner change, nor is it a strategy for inspiring the best in others. If I beat myself up internally for a perceived weakness, I am less likely to feel inspired to make positive changes and more likely to do things that aren't in my best interest. For example, if I'm trying to eat healthier and one night I eat too many cookies, if I feed (pardon the pun) the guilt with an onslaught of negative thought and self-criticism, I'm more likely to continue to overeat or possibly develop an eating disorder. Feeling terrible about ourselves leads to treating ourselves terribly, which leads to more guilt. Do you honestly think you are going to take good care of and be at peace with your whole self when you are bashing yourself all the time?

If you struggle with chronic feelings of guilt for the things you haven't done, try on the idea that you are always doing what you *can* and let that be enough for now. You are only doing what you can do right now, and at any moment you are giving what you are *actually* capable of giving. Save the guilt for sin.

Pause and Reflect: The Guilt Trap

What things do you believe you should be accomplishing that you aren't?

_____

_____

_____

_____

_____

_____

_____

_____

There are several scriptures that have sometimes been misinterpreted in a way that works against self-care, and I've often heard clients use them as a case *against* taking good care of themselves.

The Triangle of Love

The scriptures specify the greatest commandments: "And thou shalt love the Lord thy God with all thy *heart*, and with all thy soul, and with all thy mind, and with all thy strength: this is the first commandment. And the second is like unto it, namely this, Thou shalt love thy neighbour as thyself" (Mark 12:30–31; emphasis added).

I think it's really interesting that there are *three* people involved in the two greatest commandments: "Love the *Lord thy God* with all thy heart" and "love *thy neighbor* as *thyself.*" The scripture says that loving ourselves is important and that loving our neighbors is also important. If I'm taking care of myself and I feel good about myself, I have more of myself to offer to God and others. It's comforting to know that one way to interpret this powerful scripture is that *we matter in our lives* just as much as everyone else does.

What Is the Source of Your Worth?

What do we need to be doing to be someone of worth? When I ask this question, the response typically includes things like keep the commandments, be obedient and faithful, love others. Nope! Trick question! President Thomas S. Monson has said that our worth is in our capacity to become as God (see Thomas S. Monson, "Tears, Trials, Trust, Testimony," *Ensign*, September 1997, 2).

What do you have to do to have the capacity to become like God? The answer may surprise you—nothing. You don't have to *do* anything because you already have the capacity. Your worth is unchanging. It does not change whether you are obedient or disobedient, whether you're striving your hardest or not. Your access to those feelings of worth might change, but your worth per se does not change. Burnout often comes from the exhaustion

Myth: My worth is based on my righteousness and performance.
Truth: My worth is eternal, unchanging, and is not based on performance.

of trying to *prove* your worth through good behavior or excellent performance. The life-long process of *realizing* your capacity to become like God does take action on your part and does involve commitment and obedience to commandments, true conversion to Jesus Christ, learning to love—but having the capacity does not require action on your part.

Pause and Reflect: The Source of Your Worth

What have you assumed is the source of your worth?

_____

_____

_____

In what ways have you tried to prove your worth by good performance?

_____

_____

_____

If you actually believed your worth was unchanging, how might your life be different?

_____

_____

_____

Separating Worth from Performance

One of the most common sources of burnout I've seen in my own life and in my clinical work with LDS clients is the belief in conditional self-worth—

the idea that worth goes up when you're being "good," obedient, righteous, or productive and that worth goes down when you're being "bad," lazy, insensitive, or disobedient.

I once worked with a client I'll call Shelly, who struggled with the concept of separating her worth from her performance. Raised in a chaotic and unstable home, Shelly learned to survive by being the good, helpful, obedient, peacemaker in her family. After years of focusing on trying to keep her mother's rage and criticism in check by anticipating her mother's expectations, she had developed a sense of worth based solely on her ability to keep her family and her coworkers happy through anticipating and responding to their needs, but at the expense of her own happiness. Shelly came in to work with me after feeling physically and emotionally burned out. We worked together to unlink her sense of worth from her performance at home and work by first recognizing that she never felt good enough as a result of her own faulty equation. Through therapy, Shelly was able to grieve the fact that she was emotionally neglected early in her life, and she learned how to identify and value her own emotional needs and desires.

In the parable of the lost sheep, the Savior beautifully and simply illustrates that our worth is not based on our performance: "What man of you, having an hundred sheep, if he lose one of them, doth not leave the ninety and nine in the wilderness, and go after that which is lost, until he find it?" (Luke 15:4). If our worth was based on obedience, then the shepherd would have written off the lost sheep as worthless and just stayed with and tended to the ninety-nine obedient sheep. But the shepherd loves all of his sheep, even the ones who wander (which is *all* of us at some point in our lives). Jesus continues the parable, telling of the joy of the shepherd when he finds the lost sheep: "he layeth it on his shoulders, rejoicing" (Luke 15:5). The lost sheep is valuable to the shepherd.

Worth and performance mirror each other when we insist on making worth dependent on performance. If you do well on a test, your worth goes up. If you lose patience with your spouse, your worth goes down. If you sleep through sacrament meeting, your worth goes down. If you attend church every single week without fail, your worth goes up . . .

In reality, your worth is stable even when your performance varies.

Our worth as human beings is unchanging and independent of our current performance on any given day.

Worth versus Worthiness

Another problem that contributes to emotional burnout is the tendency to confuse *worthiness* with worth. Remember, the *worth* of a person never ever changes. It's who you are. You were born—therefore, you matter.

Worthiness, however, is a fluctuating state. Worthiness conveys the idea that there is a certain standard that needs to be met in order to qualify for certain opportunities; outside of the Church people might refer to worthiness as a "moral code, "dignity," or "honor." For example, in the LDS culture, we talk about young men and women being *worthy* to serve full-time missions, members being *worthy* to participate in ordinance work in LDS temples, and all faithful members knowing they must be *worthy* to receive certain blessings that God has promised.

Being worthy of something doesn't mean you are better, superior, or of greater value as a person. I like to think of it as being "qualified." For example, a potential police officer candidate must prove certain physical and mental competencies in order to prove himself or herself qualified for the job. In that sense, he or she is worthy of the job if the standards are met. But if the standards are not met, does that mean he or she is a bad person, a failure, a useless creature? Of course not. He or she simply didn't prove the ability to perform to the prescribed standards for that job at that time. If you are not "worthy" to attend the temple, it doesn't mean you are a bad person. It means you have not done what is necessary to be qualified for that opportunity right now. Don't hang your head in shame or beat yourself up. Just work on getting yourself qualified.

Feeling good about yourself and realizing your worth is always important and, in fact, plays an important role in relationships. It's very hard to connect with people who are constantly putting themselves down or dismissing the kind things others have to say. Some don't say anything out loud, but you can get the sense from their behavior or posture that they feel they have nothing good to offer. It's as though they are determined to prove that there is not a single good thing about them.

Accepting Compliments

I was gratified to learn that 50 percent of those who took my survey can easily accept compliments, but I want to talk to the 50 percent of you who have a hard time with it or who get uncomfortable when offered kind words.

People who have a hard time accepting compliments will often react by doing something dismissive. When given a compliment, have you ever:

—Laughed, scoffed.

—Rolled your eyes.

—Discounted or diminished the compliment verbally.

> **Survey: Accepting Compliments**
> 50 percent of women surveyed have difficulty accepting compliments.

—Tried to talk the giver out of the compliment: "Thanks, but really, it was not that great" or "Are you kidding? You're the one with the cute jacket!"

—Believed people were being facetious or teasing you.

—Become suspicious.

—Walked away, ignored the comment.

—Offered a meager "thanks" and walked away quickly.

If any of that sounds familiar, you might be among the 50 percent who has a hard time accepting compliments. Why is it hard to acknowledge when someone says something positive about us?

> **Workshop Comments: Accepting Compliments**
>
> Workshop participants gave the following reasons for not being able to acknowledge positive comments:
>
> - Because we say so many negative things to ourselves.
> - What they think of me doesn't fit with what I think of me.
> - They must not be talking about me.
> - If I easily accept compliments, I won't appear humble.
> - They don't know the real me.

Pause and Reflect: Accepting Compliments

When someone offers you a compliment, how do you generally respond?

_____

_____

_____

Wanting to be humble is a big reason people have a hard time accepting compliments. But it might be more accurate to say that we reject the compliment because we want people to *think* we're humble—which, ironically, is actually pride. Isn't it? It's as though we are thinking, "I don't want someone to think that I'm full of myself," which means, "I'm motivated by what other people think of me," which is pride. Recognizing the good gifts God has given you is the ultimate humility.

If you have a hard time accepting compliments from others, here is another perspective. Think about accepting a compliment as recognizing God's gifts and goodness that other people see in the creation of *you*. It's really not your fault that you have been blessed with whatever people see in you; God gave it to you! When you find yourself saying or thinking, "No, no, I'm not good at that," you are not acknowledging the talents, the gifts, and the goodness in you. And if you are not acknowledging the goodness in you, you are not acknowledging the hand of God in your life. Humility means recognizing your dependence on God for everything.

Rejecting a compliment also invalidates others for seeing what they see in you. But I've found that for many of us, our view of ourselves and our goodness is miniscule compared to what others see in us. We are the

Myth: If I notice good things about myself I am being prideful.
Truth: Gratefully acknowledging God's goodness in me is actually *humility!*

first to find reasons to belittle ourselves and point out our flaws, which makes it hard to receive any other point of view that doesn't closely match our own. Receiving a compliment can actually be a very gracious thing because you are allowing somebody to think their own thoughts about you. Try letting them have their own opinions instead of talking them out of their viewpoint. They just want to contribute to you, so accept the gift!

What if you reply to the next compliment you receive with something like, "Thank you so much. That really feels good to hear. Thanks for seeing that in me." You see, it's really about seeing what God has given you, which is everything: the breath that we breathe, the body that we have, the talents we have been blessed with, the opportunities we have been given. Saying "Thank you for seeing that in me" and accepting a compliment is not prideful. It's all a gift, and when we can't accept the positive, we're denying blessings or at least not acknowledging the blessings that God has given to us.

It's also fairly common for us as women to fall into the trap of comparing ourselves to others. We put ourselves down when we think someone else is somehow better than we are. Or we put others down to make ourselves feel better. If you are concerned about humility, consider that the habit of comparing yourself to another is the ultimate recipe for pride.

I love what C.S. Lewis said: "Pride gets no pleasure out of having something, only out of having more of it than the next man. It is the comparison that makes you proud: the pleasure of being above the rest. Once the element of competition has gone, pride has gone" (C. S. Lewis, *Mere Christianity* [New York: HarperCollins, 2001], 122).

Here is the flip side: If you compare yourself to other people and you always end up being the one who is less-than in some way, that's still pride! It's prideful because in a sense you are insisting that you know more than anyone else about how things are *supposed* to be. You must believe that you should be more of this or less than that and you have no patience or gratitude for the gift of your life. You insist that you are less than—but why? So you can get attention and sympathy and draw even more attention to yourself? To keep people around you that can bolster your self-esteem and try to convince you that you are okay? My invitation to you is to get out of the comparison trap altogether and leave the judging to the Lord. Your life will be so much more peaceful and your heart will be less burdened.

Focusing on what you *have* will always lead to gratitude. Focusing on what you think you *lack* will always lead to more lack.

"Ta Da!" List

Another way that we are unkind to ourselves is the tendency to fixate on what we perceive as missing from our day or from our lives. Are you a to-do list person? Do you usually get through everything on your list? I sure don't, but I try! Most of the things that we do every day never make it to the list, yet somehow this to-do list has become a faulty measurement of our worth based on our behavior and performance. It seems that for many of us, the more items checked off the list, the better woman, mother, wife, neighbor we think we are. This goes back to the myth that our self-worth is fluctuating or conditional.

If you cultivate the habit of valuing what you actually *did* accomplish each day, you will quickly recognize that worth isn't based on performance. Wouldn't it be amazing to acknowledge the many important contributions you made to others' lives and to your own? You can just lie in bed for five minutes at night and review the gifts the day offered you.

I suggest that you make a "Ta Da" list instead of (or if you are a list person—in addition to!) a "To Do" list. Think about the seemingly small things you do to maintain relationships. For example, a friend calls in a family crisis and you spend a half hour talking to her, offering comfort and support. That wasn't on the list of things to do, but you did it and it was important and worth acknowledging.

Was cleaning up your sick child's throw-up from the carpet and washing the sheets again on your to-do list for the day? Probably not, but it was really important. Were you the last person to change the toilet paper roll? Did you thank yourself the next time you went into the bathroom and a full roll of toilet paper was right there? Stuff like that never makes it onto my list, but it's really important. And what about opportunities that arise for reaching out to people? Those are rarely on the to-do list. How productive is it to look at your never-ending to-do list and think, *I didn't get anything done today. There are still dishes in the sink, and I didn't balance the checkbook or paint the bathroom. Blah.* Those tasks might be important, but before you slip into the realm of "overwhelmed," reflect on what you *did* do. If you're the mother of a small child it might look like this: "Picked up a toy, picked up another toy, got a sippy cup, picked up another toy, got another sippy cup, made lunch for the children, cleaned up the spilled food on the table and the floor, played with my child instead of plunking her in front of a screen, drove kids in the car eight different times, fed the baby twelve times, changed fourteen diapers. Kept my children alive for another twenty-four hours."

That stuff wasn't on your "list," but you did it, it was important, and it is part of your mission and your commitment to serve. You might even stand back and genuinely say, "Wow, that was cool!" or "Heavenly Father, thank you for all those opportunities. I did something good today."

Although you may not be able to cross off the significant things on your to-do list, there is nothing you do that is *insignificant,* and your presence matters. Offer a thank-you in the drive-through, give a smile to the grocery clerk, hold someone else's baby in sacrament meeting . . . it all matters.

Pause and Reflect: Your "Ta Da!" List

List ten things you did today, even if they seem insignificant. Pause and acknowledge your contributions.

1. _____
2. _____
3. _____
4. _____
5. _____
6. _____
7. _____
8. _____
9. _____
10. _____

Being Kind to Your Body

As I was approaching my fortieth birthday a few years ago, I noticed the effects of aging on my own body. I started reflecting on how narrowly we define beauty in our culture, and I had a desire to reframe the "body obsession" for myself and for other women. For years I've worked in my clinical practice with women who are seeking help with food obsession, weight issues, eating disorders, or compulsive eating, so personally and professionally I considered these questions:

- How do I relate with food in healthier ways?
- How can I define what beauty is for me instead of buying into the youth-obsessed culture?
- How can I better honor and value the miles I've traveled in this body?
- How can we, as a group of women, empower ourselves and others to value the changes that happen with time?

I know so few women who truly appreciate their physical bodies—and so many women suffer for most of their lives because they are at war with the body they've been given. Making peace with your body is an important part of self-care and preventing burnout.

"What Do You Most Want to Change about Yourself?"

I've asked this question to every group I've presented to for the past several years. Across the board, whether women are twenty years old or ninety, the number-one thing they wanted to change about themselves was their physical appearance—their weight!

Your Body Is an Instrument, Not an Ornament

Women seem much more likely than men to judge themselves as overweight (even when they are not), and women are also more likely to link body image with self-esteem. Have you ever felt dissatisfied with your body *without* feeling bad about yourself as a person?

The analogy of our bodies as ornaments or instruments seems to fit our personal assessment of ourselves. I think collectively we tend to see our bodies as ornaments, not instruments. An instrument is a tool that serves a particular purpose. It has a specific job to do and can do it well, especially in the right hands (in other words, *the Lord's hands*). An ornament is something decorative; its purpose is to beautify something else (like an ornament on a Christmas tree) or to draw attention to itself, but it is usually without any practical purpose.

There is nothing wrong with being interested in appearing graceful or beautiful; it's healthy to want to be attractive, to want to be your best self physically. But it becomes unhealthy when the desire is at the expense of not feeling good about ourselves and appreciating the gift of our bodies. So let's take a look at this whole business of wanting to change our bodies.

None of us has a perfect body—ornamentally or instrumentally. If you are convinced certain people do have perfect bodies, can you absolutely know they are truly grateful, happy, and peaceful? I know many people who appear to be very beautiful by our current standards but who are miserable.

If you struggle to love the gift of your physical body, try this. Stop and think about all the things your body can do that got you where you are today. Even if your knees are a little creaky or your eyes are not as clear as they used to be,

> **Survey Results:**
> **The Top Ten Things Women Want to Change Most about Themselves**
>
> 1. Lose weight
> 2. Have better self-esteem, self-confidence, self-worth
> 3. Improve organization and balance in life
> 4. Be in better physical health
> 5. Feel better spiritually
> 6. Be more patient and understanding
> 7. Have less worry and anxiety
> 8. Be more loving and charitable
> 9. Be happier
> 10. Be more outgoing

think of all the cool things your body can do. Pick up an anatomy book. It's amazing. Do you realize how many things your body orchestrates so well without any input from you? For example, it can heal a cut, change oxygen into carbon dioxide, digest your food, pump blood through all your arteries and veins, stand up and walk, blink your eyes, or coordinate the vibration of your vocal cords to produce intelligible sounds and speech. It really is so incredible to just have a body regardless of its limitations or abilities.

So next time you look in the mirror, what if you count the amazing things about your physical capabilities instead of judging how you appear? If you stop seeing yourself as an ornament, what exactly is the purpose of the instrument you have been given?

You Are Some Body!

The most severe consequence that Heavenly Father has ever given His children is to be denied ever having a body. Think about that. Many of our spirit brothers and sisters forfeited the opportunity to have a body and stopped right there. And here we are—we get bodies (albeit *imperfect* bodies), yet we spend our lives beating ourselves up and rejecting our physical appearance. Satan doesn't have a body; we have something Satan will never have. This body is a gift, an instrument, and a critical piece of our journey. Like a vehicle, we have to take care of it and respect it, but if we spend too much time obsessing over it, neglecting it, or abusing it, our lives get really out of balance.

Depending in which era you were born and where you were born, you have the "perfect" body according to cultural consensus at some point in history. I'm serious. Do some historical research and see the changes in women's bodies, and notice how the standards of fashion and acceptability and beauty constantly change. What is desirable or attractive is completely relative to the time and place in which you live.

What's Your Body Breed?

This idea might seem silly, but I find it incredibly useful! Think of your body as a certain breed of dog. Just think about it. You wouldn't choose a golden retriever and then expect it to look like a greyhound. You wouldn't shave a Saint Bernard to look like a poodle, nor would you put a collar belonging to a German shepherd on a Chihuahua. If you own a dog, it's pretty clear that you'd choose something you like, and you'd like what you chose. Well, guess what? Some of us are greyhounds, some are Saint Bernards, some are great Danes, some are Chihuahuas, and some are terriers. That's just our breed and there is nothing we can really do but accept it, appreciate it, and make the best of it!

Pause and Reflect: Your Body Breed

If you were a dog, what would your breed be?

_____

What kind of "breed" is your best friend?

_____

My husband and I went out for dinner to my favorite restaurant in downtown Salt Lake City with another couple. The wife is six-foot-three and her husband is six-foot-six. By comparison, my husband is five-foot-six and I'm five-foot-two. I thought to myself, *This is so hysterical! We are totally different body breeds!* I can't do a single thing to make myself taller. My tall friends can't cuddle up in a small chair like I can. It's just the way we are, and it's okay.

So how can we all be greyhounds—or whatever fashion is currently dictating? There are certain things about your physical body that you can't change. You can't change your toes or the length of your legs or the structure of your pelvis. You cannot change your breed!

Instead of pointing out all the ways that your body breed is not like another, ask yourself, *What is my breed, and how can I be the best body for my breed?* The goal is *not* to fit into the mold of the current cultural norm for attractiveness. After all, that "norm" keeps changing, and sooner or later it will be something entirely different.

One of my favorite scriptures to go along provides wisdom from the Lord Himself: "But the Lord said unto Samuel, Look not on his countenance, or on the height of his stature; because I have refused him: for the Lord seeth not as man seeth; for man looketh on the outward appearance, but the Lord looketh on the heart" (1 Sam. 16:7).

I had an experience in high school that dramatically changed how I saw my body. Most of us know that high school is especially brutal for girls, and I was as sensitive about my looks as most girls. I was a cheerleader during my junior and senior years of high school, so I had to wear a short cheerleader skirt. I was mortified every time I wore it because my big thighs weren't thin like those of my friends.

On September 13, 1985, I was walking to school in North Hollywood, California, with three of my cheerleader friends; we were wearing our new bright blue-and-white cheer uniforms, excited for the first football game of the season later that day. As we were walking in a crosswalk, I suddenly saw a flash of red out of the corner of my eye. In an instant, I was hit by a red car and thrown like a rag doll fifty feet down the street. The driver, who said she was blinded by the glare of the morning sun, managed to hit three out of four cheerleaders in the crosswalk! We were strewn across the whole street in front of the school.

I was afraid to open my eyes. I didn't know what had happened. Was I dead? Did I still have limbs? When I realized I was alive, the first thing I did was pull my skirt down (I had to cover my big thighs!) Thinking quickly, several guys who witnessed the accident pulled car covers off of convertibles parked on the street to keep us warm and prevent us from going into shock. One of my friends talked to me to try and keep me conscious until the ambulances and fire trucks arrived on the scene.

Luckily, there were no fatalities or life-threatening injuries resulting from the accident, but my body was in trouble. My left shoulder and my left leg were broken; my left knee was seriously injured and swollen to twice its usual size. While not as serious as my other injuries, the road rash on my bare legs from sliding on asphalt wasn't a pretty sight.

I had never given thought to my body as an instrument until that day. I couldn't walk with a broken leg, and my doctor wasn't sure what kind of damage my knee had sustained. He said, "We don't know if you'll ever be able to run. We can't see what's really going on with your knee until the swelling goes down." In light of what I had lost, I appreciated my body and its functions for the first time—until then, I hadn't appreciated how well my body had worked.

I missed the amazing things my body had been able to do. I couldn't walk for a long time or even lift my arm. I cheered at several football games sitting in a wheelchair or standing with crutches. I didn't know how amazing my body was until its abilities were temporarily taken from me. Up until that point I was just a seventeen-year-old thinking, *My thighs look so big in my cheerleading uniform! All my friends are skinnier than I am!* After the accident I found myself thinking, *I hope I can walk and run again.* It was a total shift in perspective.

I realize that my example draws on an experience of someone who is able-bodied. Many are born with or have accidents that result in individual and unique aspects of their bodies. If you have special needs or unique abilities, please determine how these principles apply to your own life.

Pause and Reflect: Your Body

What ten things are you genuinely grateful for about your body?

1. _____
2. _____
3. _____
4. _____
5. _____
6. _____
7. _____
8. _____
9. _____
10. _____

Redefining "Perfect"

Now that you've considered some of the physical aspects of your life, let's talk again about your whole self, particularly your emotional and spiritual self. If you have ever struggled with perfectionism or you've been too hard on yourself for mistakes or weaknesses, then this section is for you. It's also for those of you who think you don't make mistakes because you are already (supposedly) perfect.

Some of us spend a lot of time covering up our flaws and imperfections because we think others will look down on us—or because if we admit we have struggles, we fear it will mean we are unlovable or less valuable. We cover up our fear imperfections by trying to look perfect. But it doesn't work.

In her book, Brené Brown defines perfectionism in a way that resonates deeply with me as a "recovering" perfectionist. *Perfectionism*, she writes, "is the belief that if we live perfect, look perfect, and act perfect, we can minimize or avoid the pain of blame, judgment, and shame" (Brené Brown, *The Gifts of Imperfection: Let Go of Who You Think You're Supposed to Be and Embrace Who You Are* [Center City, MN: Hazelden, 2010], 56). According to Brown, perfectionists believe we are what we accomplish, so they please, perform, and perfect in an effort to earn self-worth. So many of us are caught in a vicious cycle of striving to be something that is unattainable. Talk about emotional burnout!

One of the most commonly quoted and seemingly often-misinterpreted scriptures regarding perfection is this one: "Be ye therefore perfect, even as your Father which is in heaven is perfect" (Matt. 5:48). We tend to interpret the word *perfect* as flawless. But the Greek word for *perfect* in the New Testament is *teleios*, which actually means ripe, whole, and complete—*not* flawless. Perfection is a "distant" objective we are moving toward all our lives and doesn't imply freedom from error (see Russell M. Nelson, "Perfection Pending," *Ensign*, November 1995, 86).

Those who try to live life without flaw (something that is humanly impossible) can experience feelings of deep failure, inadequacy, depression, and despair. The belief that we are *supposed* to live a flawless life is a setup for frustration and feelings of perpetual failure. It may be useful for Latter-day Saints to

> # Myth: I should be perfect now, and perfect means flawless.
> ## Truth: We are not required to be perfect now. We are required to turn our hearts completely to the Savior.

recognize that according to our theology, Jesus Christ was the only perfect person to walk the earth, and He offered His life as a sacrifice for all the sins of humanity. Therefore, if you think you must live a perfect/flawless life, you are actually bypassing one of the central teachings of the gospel! By attempting to rely on your own strength and merits to buy salvation you are rejecting the gift of His life and sacrifice offered on your behalf.

Another aspect of the scripture that is frequently overlooked is the context in which it is given. Earlier in the chapter, Jesus says, "Ye have heard that it hath been said, Thou shalt love thy neighbor, and hate thine enemy. But I say unto you, Love your enemies, bless them that curse you, do good to them that hate you, and pray for them which despitefully use you, and persecute you . . ." (Matt. 5:43–44). Christ is teaching about becoming perfect (ripe, whole, complete, a distant objective) in *love* like our Father in heaven, not about being flawless or never making mistakes. So you can stop apologizing for "not being perfect."

Psychotherapist John Rector offers the following perspective: "When accurately translated and understood, Christ's injunction for us to 'be ye therefore perfect even as your Father in heaven is perfect' (Matthew 5:48) represents an ideal for us to be *complete* or *fully developed* [similar to the psychological concept of self-actualization], and when read in the larger context of the chapter, Christ admonishes us to be *compassionate* . . . as part of being complete or whole" (John M. Rector, "Origins of Human Worth," *AMCAP Journal*, 30 [2006], 5).

In September 2011, President Dieter F. Uchtdorf reminded the women of Relief Society about the importance of being patient with themselves and that Heavenly Father doesn't expect them to be perfect now. He pointed out that each of us has strengths and weaknesses, saying that it's part of our mortal experience to have weaknesses—and that our loving Heavenly Father is well aware that none of us is perfect. While perfection is a long-term goal we should continue to work toward, and that one day we will achieve, He challenged each of us to be as patient and compassionate with ourselves as we are with others (see Dieter F. Uchtdorf, "Forget Me Not," *Ensign*, November 2011, 120).

So the scripture "Be ye therefore perfect" does not mean, "Be ye therefore *flawless*." It means, "Be ye therefore ripe, whole, complete, finished, fully developed." I can't help but think that if you're reading this book, you are already concerned about doing all that you can do in service of your own personal and spiritual development. So please stop beating yourself up. And will you help others to stop hurting themselves too? That state of completion is a distant goal, not an immediate result. We were never commanded to be without flaw.

Pause and Reflect: Redefining Perfect

What does it mean to *you* to be ripe, whole, and complete as a person?

_____

_____

_____

_____

How would it change your view of yourself if, instead of focusing on your flaws, you focused on your growth and development?

_____

_____

_____

God Wants a Perfect Heart

There is one body part that is frequently linked with the word *perfect* in the scriptures, and it's not your nose or your waist or your thighs. It's your heart! What Christ actually wants is our hearts. He wants us to turn our hearts to Him and to learn how to love Him, our enemies, our neighbors, *and* ourselves.

We are admonished, "Let your heart therefore be perfect with the Lord" (1 Kgs. 8:61). Let your *heart* be perfect. How do we gain a perfect (ripe, whole, complete) heart? Only through accepting the Atonement of Jesus Christ and giving our imperfect, wounded, hurt, bitter hearts to Him.

We are instructed further on what it requires to be made "perfect in Christ": "Yea, come unto Christ, and be perfected in him, and deny yourselves of all ungodliness; and if ye shall deny yourselves of all ungodliness, and love God with all your might, mind and strength, then is his grace sufficient for you, that by his grace ye may be perfect in Christ; and if by the grace of God ye are perfect in Christ, ye can in nowise deny the power of God" (Moro. 10:32).

Pause and Reflect: A Perfect Heart

What does it really mean to have a "perfect heart"?

_____

_____

_____

_____

What would it take for you to develop a more "perfect heart" and to be more "perfect in Christ"?

_____

_____

_____

_____

He Maketh My Way Perfect

Here's another scripture that has helped me to redefine "perfect": "As for God, his way is perfect; the word of the Lord is tried: he is a buckler to all them that trust in him. For who is God, save the Lord? and who is a rock, save our God? God is my strength and power: and *he maketh my way perfect*" (2 Sam. 22:31–33; emphasis added).

So what if instead of focusing on external flawlessness we focus on allowing Christ to make our *way* perfect, our path perfect, so that we are living and learning the things that we need to learn at this point in our journey? I'm not talking about a life that *looks* flawless but about a willingness to follow promptings of the Spirit and a willingness to accept the growth opportunities that we have on our journey. What if we could see that our lives provide us with the opportunities to learn what we came to earth to learn? What if we accept ourselves as we are?

One of my favorite quotes about accepting ourselves right where we are, and being gentle with our station in life at any moment, is this one:

When we plant a rose seed in the earth, we notice that it is small, but we do not criticize it as "rootless and stemless." We treat it as a seed, giving it the water and nourishment required of a seed. When it first shoots up out of the earth, we don't condemn it as immature or underdeveloped; nor do we criticize the buds for not being open when they appear. We stand in wonder at the process taking place and give the plant the care it needs at each stage of its development. The rose is a rose from the time it is a seed to the time it dies. Within it, at all times, it contains its whole potential. It seems to be constantly in the process of change; yet at each stage, at each moment, it is perfectly all right as it is. (W. Timothy Gallwey, *The Inner Game of Tennis: The Classic Guide to the Mental Side of Peak Performance* [New York: Random House, 1997], 21)

Pause and Reflect: Redefining Perfection

Describe how would you feel if you felt "perfectly all right as you are."

_____

_____

_____

_____

What would be different in your life if you realized that you are not supposed to be flawless, but that the goal is to become someone who is fully developed as a human, with a heart bound to Christ? How would that change your perspective?

_____

_____

_____

_____

_____

What might you focus your attention on if not your body or external appearance?

_____

_____

_____

_____

I really believe our lives unfold with perfect timing in order for us to learn the lessons that we need to learn. We don't criticize a little rose seed for being without stem and root; it's simply not fully developed as a mature rosebush or blossom, but it will be someday. We can see that potential in the rose—but can we see it in ourselves? We are simply not fully developed. We are not finished. We are works in progress and God gives us the experiences we need in order to continue growing.

CURE 6: LEARN TO ASK FOR AND ACCEPT HELP

A BACKPACK IS A GOOD visual representation of a burden. You know what it feels like to carry a heavy backpack; you've probably seen kids walking home from school hunched over from the weight of a huge backpack. It's hard not to want to help them. At times, all of us will carry extremely heavy burdens, whether loneliness due to the death of loved one, the stress of unemployment, the painful choices of children, or chronic mental or physical illness.

In my clinical practice, I have the honor of listening to and knowing the depth of the burdens my clients carry. Heavy emotional burdens are what bring most people into therapy in the first place. I've noticed that many clients, while completely willing to reach out to others in times of need, are reluctant to reach out for help with their own emotional pain. Let's take a look at why that might be.

Asking for Help from Others

We are told, "Bear ye one another's burdens, and so fulfill the law of Christ" (Gal. 6:2). That's pretty clear: It doesn't say bear *everybody's* burdens; it says "bear ye one another's burdens." I think that simply means we need each other. We can't do this alone.

Myth: Asking for help means I'm weak.

Truth: Asking for help and support is a strength and is necessary for preventing burnout.

There will be times when I need help and my backpack is so heavy I can't do it alone. And there will be times when I'll be strong and you'll need help and I'll be there for you. The beauty

Survey: Receiving Help
91 percent of women surveyed say it's easier to give help than to receive it.

of belonging to the Church with its wonderful organization of women in Relief Society is that we do help bear one another's burdens. That is at the core of *Relief* Society—bringing relief to others.

Pause and Reflect: Asking For Help

Is it easy or hard for you to ask for help? _____

Why do you think 91 percent of women find it harder to receive help than to give it?

_____

_____

_____

_____

What are your own reasons?

_____

_____

_____

_____

Do you have the mistaken idea that asking for and receiving help from others makes you look weak? There's another pride snag! Pride is about the comparison. If you compare yourself to another person and you measure above her, that's a form of pride. I believe that if you compare yourself to another person and you measure *below* her, that's *also* a form of pride. Remember that when you're motivated by where you fall in comparison to others—whether you rank above or below—it's pride. Pride *keeps you* from being humble and asking for help when you need it because you don't want to look weak.

Here are the facts: We are all weak, and we all need each other to help bear the pain and sorrow of life. Everybody falls apart and sobs in a heap at some point in life, more than once.

Part of this equation is the strong, positive belief that as individuals, couples, and families, we should be independent and self-reliant. We should all strive to be as independent and self-reliant as we can be. That does not mean, however, that we won't need some help along the way.

Not asking for help or accepting help leads you into that overwhelmed, exhausted place! Part of preventing burnout is learning to ask for help; if you don't, you are denying other people the blessing of serving you. There is no greater gift than someone gratefully accepting service. I'll say it again—there is no greater contribution you can

> **Workshop Comments: Receiving Help**
>
> Why is it so hard for women to ask for and receive help? My workshop participants said:
> —I have to reach a point of total desperation before I ask for help.
> —It makes us look weak.
> —I don't want to burden anyone else with my problems.
> —I really ought to be able to handle everything in my life on my own.
> —If I can't handle things myself, it's like admitting that I am not deserving of the things I have, like my kids, and my other responsibilities; it's like I'm incapable or unworthy.

make to another than to *allow them* to contribute to you! If it's important for each to serve but nobody is willing to be served, then we all miss out on the opportunity to make a difference for each other.

Do you realize the irony? One of ways you can actually help, nurture, and serve others is to *allow* others to serve you. You might think, *I'll be fine if I can just look like I have it all together and make sure it appears to others that my family is fine.* Well, you can only fake it for so long. What if instead you had the courage to say, "I'm not fine. I need somebody to talk to." Or, "I'm not fine. I just found out my husband lost his job and I'm heartbroken." Or, "I'm not fine. I'm totally depressed. I don't want to get out of bed."

Someone needs to be willing to receive the service that others want to offer. If not, opportunities are lost for blessings on both sides.

As a whole, if we want to really thrive in life and prevent burnout, we have to get better at asking and accepting help when we need it. We're all in the same boat. We all desperately need each other and we all desperately need the Savior. You may believe that everybody else has it all together, but I promise you, nobody does. *Nobody* does. That's one thing I love about my profession. I see the inside of people's lives, not just what they want others to see on the outside. It's the real deal.

Pause and Reflect: When I've Needed Help

Think of a time when you've needed help physically, intellectually, emotionally, spiritually, or practically. How did you let others know of your need?

_____

_____

_____

_____

If you did ask someone for help, how did that person respond to your request?

_____

_____

_____

_____

If you weren't able to reach out and ask for help, what beliefs or fears prevented you from doing so?

_____

_____

_____

_____

List five times you were able to help someone.

1. _____

2. _____

3. _____

4. _____

5. _____

What emotions did you feel as you were giving help? How did you feel toward the person you were serving?

_____

_____

_____

_____

List five times someone helped you in a time of need.

1. _____

2. _____

3. _____

4. _____

5. _____

How do you imagine that person felt as he or she offered help to you? How did you feel toward the person serving you?

_____

_____

_____

_____

Asking for Professional Help

Asking for help may mean asking for professional help. Unfortunately, there are still looming stigmas and myths about seeing a counselor or a therapist, and those beliefs are often reinforced when you judge yourself and others for having mental health problems or for needing professional help. For example, someone might say, "If you were ___(fill in the blank)___, your kid wouldn't be on drugs or you wouldn't have depression or anxiety." Would you say that to somebody who had asthma? Would you say, "You know, you'd be able to breathe better if you read your scriptures more." Of course not. But somehow, mental, emotional, and relationship problems seem to be fair game for unfair judgment.

Part of my motivation in doing workshops is to encourage women to "get real" about what's going on in their lives. I hope that providing actual statistics will help free up some communication about the struggles individuals and families are facing.

Myth: Going to counseling is a sign of spiritual or personal weakness.

Truth: Everyone can benefit from an outside perspective during difficult times; therapy can even make a good thing better!

Here are the top three reasons why those who sought professional help or counseling did so:

1. Depression. The most common answer was depression, which is a broad category with many dimensions; if you're struggling with any aspect of depression, you are not alone!

2. Marriage problems. Having marriage issues is normal. It doesn't mean that you are bad or broken. Nobody has a flawless marriage, and conflict is a normal part of putting two people together. Couples can learn how to skillfully weather all kinds of storms and grow closer together.

3. Family issues/children. That's no surprise—we tend to pull out all the stops when our family is being threatened by unworkable patterns and behaviors. Whether it's your own spouse or children or the family you were born into, we all experience pain and disappointment at some time.

Survey: Emotional and Mental Health

—64 percent of women surveyed have *personally* struggled with emotional or mental health problems.
—31 percent of women surveyed have gone to counseling.

Survey Results: Top 10 Reasons LDS Women Seek Professional Counseling

1. Depression
2. Marriage counseling
3. Family and children
4. Anxiety
5. Death or grief
6. Self-esteem
7. Abuse
8. Childhood problems or sexual abuse
9. Eating disorder
10. Postpartum depression or "baby blues"

As the survey results indicate, many women have taken the opportunity to see a professional counselor. Seeing a therapist is not a sign of weakness! It is a sign that you are committed to your ongoing growth and realize you can benefit from an outside perspective.

You don't have to have big problems to see a therapist. Many people who are otherwise dealing well with their life choose to see a therapist to help them stay on track or be proactive about emerging issues. Parents who are concerned about their parenting skills can work with a therapist to learn how to better meet the needs of their children. Couples who are having minor conflict don't have to wait to seek therapy until divorce is looming! Even Olympic athletes who are the best of the best have coaches who help them maintain world-class performance. There are many reasons to reach out for professional support—it doesn't mean you have something "wrong" in your life. Don't wait until your life falls apart!

Counseling Mentioned by LDS Leaders

Since I am a therapist, you won't be surprised to learn that I listen closely in general conference for mentions of professional counseling by the general authorities. I am glad when I hear counseling offered as an avenue for healing of emotional and relationship problems. Knowing the shame that many individuals feel about seeking counseling, and also knowing how many people benefit from it, I'm encouraged by official acknowledgment of counseling from Church leaders because it makes it easier for people to seek professional help.

Elder Jeffrey R. Holland, in referring to sexual sins, counseled that people often need more help than they can provide themselves. He encouraged listeners to seek help in the form of a bishop's counsel, a priesthood blessing, LDS Family Services, other suitable professional help, and prayer, through which we are entitled to ask angels to help us (see Jeffrey R. Holland, "Place No More for the Enemy of My Soul," *Ensign*, May 2010, 45).

In the same conference, Elder Wilford W. Andersen of the Second Quorum of the Seventy acknowledged the reality of depression and anxiety. Along with encouraging us to seek help from competent professionals, he urged us to place our trust in the Savior, who is the Prince of Peace (see Wilford W. Andersen, "The Rock of Our Redeemer," *Ensign*, May 2010, 17).

Of the consequences of abuse, Elder Richard G. Scott pointed out that no one would attempt to fix a broken leg by himself or herself. He urged us to seek help from a thoughtful bishop or stake president or a wise professional counselor, and emphasized that complete healing comes from the Savior (see Richard G. Scott, "To Heal the Shattering Consequences of Abuse," *Ensign*, May 2008, 42).

Barriers to Seeking Professional Counseling

If you have ever thought to seek professional help and have not followed through, consider your reasons. Is it pride? Is it a belief that your problems can't be helped? Is it a lack of time or money or trusted counselors? You may not be surprised that I have solutions to all of the top six reasons or excuses for not seeking counseling when you need it.

Top 6 Reasons Latter-Day Saints Who Need Counseling Don't Follow Through—and Some Suggestions

Money

If you have health insurance, check on your mental health benefits. For many insurance plans, it's about the same as the copay for a visit to your family physician. You might also check with your bishop about your needs. He may be able to help financially.

Look for sliding-scale clinics.

Check with local colleges and universities for low-cost therapy options offered by graduate students in training.

Time

Choose to cut your weekly TV or Internet time in half. You'll find the time for counseling.

Everyone has twenty-four hours in a day. We make time for the things we value most. Many therapists have hours available very early and very late in the day to accommodate people's busy schedules.

Embarrassment

Remember that nearly one-third of women surveyed have gone to counseling. Look around in your church meetings next week and remember that every third person sitting there has seen a counselor. Welcome the experience and embrace it as you would any self-improvement activity or investment.

Thinking You Can Fix It Yourself

If you could have fixed it yourself, you would have. All too often I hear people say, "I wish I had sought help sooner."

Not Knowing Where to Go

Talk to your Church leaders and ask for recommendations. Ask your close friends and family members for referrals; many of them have gone to counseling.

Your Spouse Doesn't Support You

What would you do if you had cancer and your spouse didn't support your treatment? At some point, you have to take responsibility for yourself and for getting your needs met. If you really need marriage counseling and your spouse won't go, go by yourself. Many times I've met with a wife alone; after she starts doing better, her husband wants to start coming to therapy.

Mental Health and Relationship Counseling Resources

If money is a barrier to seeking counseling, many mental health and family therapy clinics have sliding-fee scales based on income. Some also offer free counseling. Universities with graduate programs for therapists sometimes offer counseling for free from the graduate school candidates. Also be sure to determine whether mental health benefits are offered by your health insurance.

Regardless of where you live, you ought to be able to find similar resources. Even if you're in a relatively isolated area, many therapists offer remote services such as phone, e-mail, and video conferencing.

Talk to your bishop; he can help you make use of the plentiful and excellent resources offered through LDS Social Services. There's also a great resource called ldscounselors.net that consists of therapists who identify themselves as LDS and who live all over the world.

The point is, don't let anything get in the way of getting the support you need.

Ask for Help from the Savior

Another common misconception that contributes to burnout is the belief that you aren't able to access Christ's help and His grace until after you've done everything you can do. I've heard clients say, "I'm so imperfect. I haven't done all I can do, so how can I ask the Lord for help? The scriptures tell us that Christ will save us only *after* all we can do, right?"

> # Myth: Christ will help me only after I've done everything I can.
> # Truth: Christ will help us all along the way.

I believe that "after all we can do" (2 Ne. 25:23) can be applied to our lives in at least a couple of different ways. First, the grace by which we are saved after all we can do refers to our eternal salvation at the end of our mortal existence.

An additional way this scripture can be understood is in reference to our daily lives—meaning that while God requires our heart and our best effort to be obedient to His commandments, we are saved by His grace continually throughout our natural life. In his book, *The Broken Heart*, Elder Bruce C. Hafen suggests that "the Savior's gift of grace to us is not necessarily limited to 'after' all we can do. We may receive his grace before, during, and after the time when we expend our own efforts" (Bruce C. Hafen, *The Broken Heart:*

Applying the Atonement to Life's Experiences [Salt Lake City: Deseret Book, 1989], 155–156). This helps us understand that grace can be a continual source of spiritual strength.

Let's look at the entire verse: "For we labor diligently to write, to persuade our children, and also our brethren, to believe Christ, and to be reconciled to God; for we know that it is by grace that we are saved, after all we can do" (2 Ne. 25:23).

I find it more helpful to understand this scripture for our daily lives as "in addition to" all we can do, instead of "after" all we can do—a set time frame. The footnote on the word *do* points to "good works" in the Topical Guide. When will we be done doing all of the good works we can do? Not for a very long time—probably not ever!

Jesus invites us to partake of His rest now—as in, *today, tomorrow,* and *always*: "Come unto me, all ye that labour and are heavy laden, and I will give you rest. Take my yoke upon you, and learn of me; for I am meek and lowly in heart: and ye shall find rest unto your souls. For my yoke is easy, and my burden is light" (Matt. 11:28–30).

Turn Your Burden Over to the Lord

We appreciate the ideas of repentance and forgiveness but we might have a hard time doing the actual physical, mental, emotional, and spiritual work that is required to achieve them. This is connected directly to the difficulty we sometimes have with the process of turning our burdens over to the Lord; it is appealing but equally as challenging in practice. What follows are some real-life stories of women who, by drawing on the power of the Atonement, have turned their burdens over to the Savior. It is my hope that reading their stories of triumph and healing will help illustrate how it can be done and that the Lord is there for you in your time of need. (The names of these women have been changed to protect their privacy.)

Sandra

I find solace in reading my scriptures and attending the temple. Only there can I find the peace and love I have so desperately needed since my son's death in Afghanistan. The song "Where Can I Turn for Peace" says it all for me. There have been times I did not get out of bed or take a shower for three days in a row. As I pondered the meaning of life and wondered if I even wanted to keep living, I found that the love of the Savior was the only thing that pulled me through the darkest of my days. I was given the prompting to begin speaking at public events about my amazing son and his life of integrity. I found the more I focused on my loss, the more sadness crept into my soul, but once I started speaking about how wonderful my son was and how he exemplified the Savior's example in his life and service to his country, the more my heart began to fill with peace and joy. Now I am asked to speak often and not only has it changed my life for the better, but I hope it instills joy in the lives of others.

Marian

When I was twenty-one, my husband of only eleven months left me to pursue his addiction to pornography. What I thought was a worthy temple marriage to a righteous returned missionary proved to be a sham. I felt utterly alone, not having many friends in a new place and being across the country from family. I felt entirely alone and emotionally devastated. I had no motivation to pick up and start over. I grieved the caring man I knew was inside this person who'd been taken over by darkness. I remember distinctly one morning trying to get ready for the day. Looking around at our apartment the pain came on to me all at once like a wave. I found myself sobbing uncontrollably on the bath mat. I thought to myself how no one could even hear me and that there was no one within hundreds of miles who would even care.

I cried out to my Heavenly Father in agony to please fill this unbearable emptiness of pain in my heart. As I sobbed, I felt His literal arms around me. I felt Him call me *daughter* and lift me up. I felt Him wipe my tears. I knew without a shadow of a doubt in that moment that I was not alone and that His love was real. I knew it was by no power of my own that I was calming down and the pain was subsiding.

As I continued throughout that day and the hard years that followed, I knew it was Him holding me up. When others remarked of my strength, I bore my testimony that I was not doing it alone. God's love for us and the power of the Atonement is real and literal. In our emotional pain we can call out to a Father and a Brother, our Savior, who have powers beyond our understanding. He is waiting with His literal arms stretched out to hold us in our agony. He can make our burdens light. I know because I've felt it.

Jessica

The only reason I have hope to be happy is because of the Atonement of Jesus Christ. My father left me and my younger brother when I was three years old when my parents divorced. We only visited him twice growing up. My mother was mentally ill, addicted to drugs, and was both neglectful and abusive. I was pretty much the adult in charge at home from the time I was eight years old. I raised my brother, my sister, and my mother. The pain of being abandoned, the anger at my abusive mother, and the sheer loneliness was overwhelming. I didn't have friends, neighbors, aunts, uncles, or cousins. The only person on the planet that I knew loved me was my father's mother, who lived in another state. Nobody cared if we ate every day, had warm clothes in the winter, or even attended school. Nobody really had time to realize we were even there, since we moved at least once a year. I attended thirteen schools.

The year I was a Sunbeam, my family went to church. My teacher taught me how to pray. I prayed and prayed and prayed. I prayed when I was sad, lonely, or afraid. . . . which was daily. I felt the Spirit, and I knew that I was a child of God.

When I was fourteen, we moved to Utah. Finally, I could walk to church! I dragged my brother and sister kicking and screaming. I attended seminary and had wonderful teachers, Young Women leaders, and bishops who took an interest in me. My junior year of high school, I determined that it didn't matter if a single person on the planet cared about me, because I would care about me. I started attending school and taking AP classes and raised my GPA from 1.4 to a 3.4. I worked two jobs to support myself, volunteered in the community, served as Laurel class president, and did a lot of extracurricular activities. I even went to seminary summer school so I could graduate with a four-year certificate instead of a three-year certificate.

Giving all my hurt, all my disappointment, and all my pain to Christ allowed me to forgive my parents, repent of my sins, and have peace in my heart. I can honestly say that I have completely forgiven my parents and that I am full of gratitude for all of my blessings.

<u>Emily</u>

Five years ago I was addicted and felt desperately small and alone in this world. My unmanageable life was on a fast track for ruining every relationship I had. With nothing left, I began to pray for change. Please get me through this moment, I would plead, and then I would pray again, get me through this moment, and then I would pray again. I prayed in the morning, in the car, as I worked; I begged my Father to bless His broken daughter and guide my troubled steps. It seemed my life was a constant prayer to ease the pain I felt and give me courage for the changes I needed to make.

I look back on that time and I am amazed at the goodness of my Father's love for me. His Spirit was my constant companion when I finally turned to find Him. He didn't wait until I deserved His love. He didn't wait until my life was perfect. He showed up while I still struggled with sin and addiction. Over the months and years that followed I developed a relationship with God. He is my comfort as I make my way through the life I live. I lay my burdens at His feet when they are too heavy to carry.

Joanne

When we lost our youngest son in an accident, I found that I absolutely had to turn my burdens over to the Savior. Through music and the scriptures, I was able to feel His love . . . His arms around me.

Carmen

I have found peace by coming unto Him and recognizing that He too has felt what I am feeling. He was perfect, but that did not mean He didn't feel pain, or stress, or loneliness. When I have feelings of inadequacy, it's often because I am not drawing close to the Lord like I need to. Satan gets in there and tugs at my soul; he knows my weaknesses. When I have feelings of loneliness, I know that my Savior loves me. I can feel Him embrace me. Around the holidays, my loneliness increases. I feel sorry for myself that I don't have a family of my own, and when I watch those sappy holiday shows, I often wonder where my eternal mate is. I decided that when those feelings of loneliness occur, I am going to step outside myself and serve others. I try to see others and love others the way He does.

Tamara

I am in the process of a heartbreaking divorce completely not of my choosing. At times things have truly been too heavy to bear. I plead with the Savior to lighten my load. Many times I've felt the heavy weight lifted and a beautiful peace floods my soul. The healing balm of the Atonement heals despair, doubt, deceit, and loneliness. In times of my most private heartbreak and sense of aloneness, I know I am not alone. He has chosen to walk this unknown road with me. He has felt the pain that pierces my heart until I am sure it will break. He is there to help me to keep moving forward instead of being paralyzed by fear. He encourages me to choose faith.

My Own Story . . .

There was a time a few years ago when I was feeling totally burned out, overwhelmed, overextended, and spiritually numb. We had just moved to a new home after living in the same area for more than a decade. I had just had my third baby and was having difficulty adjusting to having children in all different stages of life. Between family life and my therapy practice, I had little time or inclination to write songs, and I felt a lack of "spark" and passion in my life. Writing songs is a primary way that I work through difficult emotions and seek answers to my heart's longings, but I felt empty and uninspired.

At this same time—maybe it had something to do with the realities of aging—I was feeling a void in my ability to apply the gospel to my "real" life, day in and day out. I wasn't partaking of the joy, the depth, and the "good news" of the gospel as I knew I could.

As I read and pondered the life of Christ and marveled at the miracles of His earthly ministry, I remember thinking, *It must have been really great to witness the miracle, but what does that have to do with my life right now?* And as I thought about it, I had one of those—or several of those—moments where I "got it." Oprah Winfrey calls them "aha moments." All of the miracles in the life of Christ are figural and literal metaphors for what He can do for me now—*today*. There are times when I need to be raised from spiritual death or emotional death. There are times when my eyes aren't seeing clearly, where I'm blinded by pride or by sin. There are times when I'm not listening to the Spirit, and my ears need to be opened.

There are times when I feel like I don't have what it takes to meet the demands of my life and my relationships. It's like I have just a few loaves and fishes and there are so many hungry people that want and need them. What I realized through the process of studying and writing is that if the Lord can take a few loaves and fishes and feed a multitude, then He can take whatever we have to offer and make enough of us to go around, enough to do His will, enough to develop ourselves so we have that to offer our loved ones.

His power can heal our blindness, open our ears, soften our hearts, and lift us to a higher plane where we are able to do the work He wants us to do.

Make Enough of Me

Overwhelmed and underpaid
Morning comes too soon
Running late and on my plate
A million things to do

Got a baby cryin'
Another trying to find the other shoe
When I open my eyes
The dam will break
Their need will flood my room

CHORUS
You made wine from water
And raised up Jairus's daughter from her bed
Filled the empty fishing nets
And with some loaves and fishes fed

A hungry crowd
Make enough of me to go around

My mother's sick
I'm late to pick up kids at school
I need to clean
Can't fit in my jeans
The fridge gives no comfort food

Multiply and magnify
This tiny little life of mine
Enlarge me
And expand this heart
And fill it with divine
My heart is cold
Nothing grows
But thistles and some thorns
They choke the light
And shrink the vine
I need to be reborn
You made wine from water
And told a scarlet daughter
Sin no more
Surrendered to the garden
Through thorns and nails you pardoned
The angry crowd
Make enough of me to go around.

(Lyrics by Julie de Azevedo; © 2005 Julie de Azevedo (BMI),
from the album *Masterpiece: The Best of Julie de Azevedo*)

When I place my life in God's hands, trust in the Lord's promises, and
listen to the whisperings of the Spirit to guide me, I am able to serve others
and accomplish things that are well beyond my own capabilities. Coming to
know the Savior's love and the power of the Atonement to make me whole
is the key to preventing—and maybe even curing—burnout in my own life
and finding relief from feeling overwhelmed, sad, lost, inadequate, and alone.

I believe that He allows us to struggle with limitations and weaknesses so
we may be humble, learn faith, and experience the grace as promised in the
scriptures: "Then will I make weak things become strong unto them" (Ether

12:27). I believe that He wants us to understand ourselves, value ourselves, take good care of ourselves, and treat ourselves as kindly as we treat others. I believe that He wants us to trust in Him and the power of His Son's Atonement to lift our burdens. I believe that God wants us to have joy. I believe He wants us to take good care of ourselves so we have a joyful and loving self to offer in His service. *We* are His work and His glory.

Some Conclusions and Reminders

We have tools to help us become the amazing women God intended us to be. We have living prophets and apostles, the gift of the Holy Ghost, the scriptures, the priesthood, and personal revelation to guide us. We also have emotional signals that steer us and teach us about what we value, what we want. We are women with a majestic heritage and a bright and vital role in building up the kingdom of God on earth. Our work must be founded on a firm and faithful conviction as infinitely unique individuals; our souls are of great worth to God. This foundational and faithful relationship with God informs and inspires not only our own lives, but also the interpersonal relationships we have with others as an integral aspect of the good news of the gospel.

My sincere hope is that this book has helped, and will continue to help you seek spiritual guidance from divine sources as you develop a greater sense of emotional awareness and self-compassion that strengthens and amplifies your ability to serve and care for others. When we treat ourselves kindly, accept (and work to improve) our personal limitations, and discover our individual missions, we can claim the joy that is ours. When we are overflowing with joy and love, this goodness will emanate from deep within our souls. As we become more complete and healthy, there will be more of ourselves to give to and share with others. However, this ability to be an efficient and effective instrument in the Lord's hands also requires continual investment in and responsibility for our own growth.

As wonderful as it might be, finishing this book will not magically make the trials in your life disappear. Everyone struggles in this life, but struggle can equal growth. I pray that as you complete this book you will continue to contemplate and cultivate a view of life that focuses on Christ as the center of our energy and efforts. The Savior's infinite Atonement strengthens us and buoys us up in the tempestuous sea of life as we seek to do His will. In the process of being and becoming Christ-like, we need genuine connections with other sisters to buoy each other up during this difficult mortal journey.

Pause and Reflect: Turning Your Burdens Over to the Lord

Now it's your turn. Think of a time when you felt the strength of the Savior lighten your burden. Describe your experience in as much detail as possible.

_____

_____

_____

_____

_____

_____

What burdens, worries, or concerns are you carrying right now?

_____

_____

_____

_____

List any thoughts, feelings, or beliefs that are preventing you from turning your burdens over to the Lord today.

_____

_____

_____

_____

What specific help do you need from the Savior right now?

_____

_____

_____

_____

_____

ABOUT THE AUTHOR

JULIE DE AZEVEDO HANKS, MSW, LCSW, is a self-care and relationship expert, media contributor, blogger, speaker, songwriter, and licensed therapist with twenty years of experience counseling LDS women, couples, and families. In addition to owning Wasatch Family Therapy, LLC, and serving as executive director, Hanks is an emotional health and relationship expert on TV and radio. She is a regular contributor on KSL TV's Studio 5 and has appeared nationally on TLC, Discovery Health, and FOX News Channel. Her down-to-earth advice has also been featured in *The Wall Street Journal, Cosmopolitan, CNN, Women's Day, Women's Health, Real Simple, Parenting,* and others. Hanks writes for Answers, Sharecare, DailyStrength, and PsychCentral websites.

As an award-winning performing songwriter, Julie de Azevedo has written dozens of songs, contributed to numerous projects, and produced ten solo CDs over the past twenty-five years. Her most recent CD, *Masterpiece: The Best of Julie de Azevedo,* is a collection of her best-loved songs.

Hanks's most valuable experience has been "in the trenches" of family life as a wife to Jeff Hanks and mother of four children. In her "spare time," Hanks is earning her PhD in marriage and family therapy, taking long naps, and eating a lot of chocolate.

For additional emotional health, self-care, and relationship resources, visit JulieHanks.com.